The Hodder Book of Prayers in Large Print

The Hodder Book of Prayers in Large Print

Compiled by Rosemary Curtis
With a foreword by the Archbishop of York

Dear Readers, from this rhyme take warning,
And if you heard the bell this morning
Your Vicar went to pray for you,
A task the Prayer Book bids him do.
'Highness' or 'Lowness' do not matter,
You are the Church and must not scatter,
Cling to the Sacraments and pray
And God be with you every day.

John Betjeman

Hodder & Stoughton
LONDON SYDNEY AUCKLAND

Compilation copyright Rosemary Curtis 1997

First published in Great Britain 1997

10 9 8 7 6 5 4 3 2 1

British Library Cataloguing in Publication Data
A record for this book is available from the British Library

ISBN 0 340 69411 4

Typeset by Hewer Text Composition Services, Edinburgh
Printed and bound in Great Britain by
Clays Ltd, St Ives plc

Hodder & Stoughton Ltd
A Division of Hodder Headline PLC
338 Euston Road
London NW1 3BH

I dedicate this book to my children
and a lighthouse keeper

May your lamps burn brightly

Acknowledgments

Without the loving help of the following people, including the Presidents of Churches Together in England, most Catholic and Anglican Diocesan Bishops, and many others too numerous to mention, this book may not have been possible: the Rt Revd John Austin Baker, former Bishop of Salisbury, who encouraged the germination of the Churches and Blindness; the Bishop of Hereford and the Bishop of Taunton (Bishop Designate of St Edmundsbury and Ipswich) in the frightening moments; Robert Willis, now Dean of Hereford, whose ministry in Sherborne enabled so much to follow; Sir Harry Secombe CBE; Rear Admiral Sir John Garnier KCVO, CBE; Robert Webb, SPCK Salisbury for his unstinting support and also Brian Shelswell and William Cole both of SPCK; Alison White and colleagues at the Mitchell Library, Glasgow; Jane Starling, Communications Officer of the Scottish Episcopal Church, Edinburgh; The Revd Maxwell Craig, General Secretary Action of Churches Together in Scotland and Shona Denham; staff and students of Yeovil College especially the Department of Information Technology; Yeovil Reference Library; Sister Angela Helen CSF; the Revd Father Anthony OSB; Len and Sheila Flint together with Lexmark International for always going and giving the extra mile! Sun Life Assurance Society, Bristol for donating a replacement computer on 21 December 1996; Ted Ashley for making a lectern which made learning braille (with sight) infinitely easier, and many friends who prayed daily for the project's progress, their respite care, and gifts; the Revd Canon Martin Reardon, General Secretary of Churches Together in England with Bishop Peter Firth (Chairman) and the Bishop of Clifton and the Steering Group; Mark Robinson MP and the Employment Service; Mrs Monica Cole of Catus, France; Mr Lawrence Mitchell; Clive Waring-Flood; the clergy and staff of Sherborne Abbey, Dorset. Mr Geoff David for courage and kindness way above normal banking! Staff in London at Church House, Vaughan House, and Central Hall; the Guide and Scout Associations for the 1995 Church Survey; the people, circuits and parishes of Weymouth, Dorset; Graham Winterbourne and Dodd Briggs for their dedication and expertise; and countless blind and partially sighted people and the respective caring organisations.

My great gratitude to Emma Sealey for editorial guidance and for the joyful privilege of compiling the anthology, is unending.

Contents

Foreword By the Archbishop of York

Though this publication is deliberately of light weight, so as to enable its ease of handling by the arthritic and elderly, spiritually it is a heavy-weight because of the sheer breadth and depth of its contents. There is much wisdom here. D.H. Lawrence surprises us by ably addressing sleep, disability and death in one line: '[God] is breaking me down to his own oblivion, to send me forth on a new morning'. If the prayer 'Children learn what they live' were taken to heart by our society, most of the present concerns about parenting and education would be solved at a stroke. On the subject of children, the inclusion of details of the service following the Dunblane massacre is a worthy one, especially for Rabindranath Tagore's line: 'Death is not the extinguishing of the light, but the putting out of the lamp, because Dawn has come.'

There is always a danger that such anthologies may veer towards a syrupy sentimentality, pulling out all the stops to engender a spiritual feel-good factor. This collection is redeemed from that fault by not being afraid to be hard-hitting, not least to those who suffer, quoting the seventeenth-century Nun's Prayer: 'Lord, keep me reasonably sweet ... a sour old person is one of the crowning works of the devil.' Bishops are also kept in their place, as Steve Turner's meditation on Christmas exemplifies: 'Let's award him [Jesus] a degree in theology, a purple cassock and a position of respect. They'll never think of looking there.'

The large-print and clear presentation is particularly aimed at the partially-sighted. Yet the genius of this book is that many of its prayers illustrate how we are all near blind when it comes to faith. We are driven to pause, and, with R.S. Thomas, find that 'the meaning is in the waiting'. I congratulate the author and the publishers on such an excellent venture, and pray that all of us, who have waiting so inconveniently thrust upon us, find God therein.

David Ebor
Summer 1997

Introduction

A lifelong Anglican, I owe my ecumenical roots to my grandparents and parents – a Congregationalist father and an Anglican mother – who married in 1934. They worshipped on alternate weeks in the little village church or in the Congregational church in Addison Street, Nottingham, until the introduction of petrol rationing in the Second World War prevented that practice. I would have fallen apart if I had lived my life separated from God. Instead, as each event or challenge came along, the more I drew on God, my faith and his love in it.

Faith is a gift from God but it needs nurturing especially when the foundation stones of our lives are being laid. To have had a childhood where faith was seen and felt and was shared gave my faith a greater chance of maturing in the years ahead.

This is an ecumenical collection of prayers, for several reasons: example and conviction, but far more importantly, because there is no other large-print anthology of its kind. Therefore some readers will find that the book contains prayers, practices or even celebrations which are unfamiliar to them. We seek their understanding. For if the prayers are to make life easier for people in an age range from thirteen to a hundred – and who may include the clergy – it is inevitable that the choice must be wide.

There is a sense too that our churchmanship may change, and what once appeared unhelpful or unfamiliar in our public worship or private prayer may gradually, or suddenly, bring a freshness to it. It has been so for me. Listening to prayers on audio tape denies privacy, a book such as this enables privacy. It is my hope that these prayers will bring joy to most people.

The book's design is unique and stems from the spring of 1994. I telephoned John Rees from Arthritis Care because research had already revealed that five key subjects – ecumenical prayers, spirituality, theology, Christian ethics, and comparative religions – were largely absent in large print for purchase or loan, apart from the (marvellous) international ministry of Torch Trust for the Blind, whose address is at the back of this book. Therefore guidelines on weight restriction and the shape of the book were needed in order to minimise the pain experienced by arthritis sufferers or those coping with weak muscles from muscular dystrophy, MS, AIDS, stroke and burn victims or amputees, who also may have impaired sight. When John told me that no national survey of books for all impaired people had been undertaken, we compiled a new large-print criteria on the spot, betwixt Hampshire and Dorset. That was the easy bit!

Though my primary concern was for partially-sighted readers, born from my own brief experience of impaired vision, I should have been foolish to have ignored the needs of so many others. So, the book's weight has been restricted to eleven ounces (about a third of a kilo), while its *inner cover* is of non-slip material. The sewn binding means it will remain open at the desired page once it has been gently broken in. The paper is white – and will remain so as it is acid free – and it is of sufficient weight (thickness) to prevent shadowing from the previous page. There is excellent contrast with the bold, large fount which is deliberately plain and easy to read (sans serif). The book will be widely available.

Numerous people will be indebted to Hodder and Stoughton for their courage to be the first commercial publishers to undertake such a venture, especially in the present economic climate.

The benefit of public and private prayer

As Dr Ruth Etchells says in the introduction to her book, *Just As I Am*, ' . . . this personal dialogue with God is the very oxygen of our spiritual blood-stream, and without it we grow faint on the pilgrimage'. It does not matter where we are, or when, or who we are – God hears us. But do we know how to start praying? Do we always hear him, his encouragement, his forgiveness? Can we accept that sometimes we hear him through others?

Simone Weil (twentieth century): 'I heard by chance of the existence of the English poets of the seventeenth century who are named metaphysical. I discovered the poem . . . called 'Love'. I learnt it by heart. Often . . . I make myself say it all over, concentrating all my attention upon it, and clinging with all my soul to the tenderness it enshrines. I used to think I was merely reciting it as a beautiful poem, but without my knowing it the recitation had the virtue of prayer. It was during one of these recitations that, as I told you, Christ himself came down and took possession of me.

'Until last September I had never once prayed to God in all my life.'

The Benedictine Rule

Innumerable people – clergy and laity – have helped me on the pilgrim's way, but the Lenten Addresses in 1992 from the vicar and curates, following Compline in Sherborne Abbey – once a Benedictine Monastery – were particularly beneficial. They were on the Benedictine Rule.

St Benedict lived in sixth-century Italy and wrote his Rule for those joining the Order. But much of what St Benedict wrote is as useful today as it was almost fifteen hundred years ago: for the religious, the clergy, as well as the laity.

Benedictine Spirituality

The Rule of St Benedict is an invitation to go deeper into mystery.

The Rule itself is rooted in the Scriptures of both the Old and New Testaments. Benedict repeatedly points to Christ and His message – 'Listen to Him' and 'Learn from Him'. It's a way of life – freely embraced and joyfully received.

The first word of the Prologue sets the tone, 'Listen'. The spiritual life of a Benedictine monastic is centred on the art of listening. In such a busy and crowded life it is important to take time and to listen to the silence, to listen with one's heart and mind to the gentle whispered voice of Him who calls us together. Listening is not a passive undertaking, but an action which gradually leads the individual to a deeper understanding and appreciation of life, life lived in relation to others.

The Benedictine spirituality is also marked by vows – promises made to God before the community of believers. These vows are not seen as restrictions placed on an individual – but as ways of proclaiming our desire continually to seek the Lord.

The vow of conversion of life is an invitation to look upon the Lord and His Gospel message and to focus more directly on the essential of our graced existence. Christ is our model, the one who calls us to centre ourselves on Him – thus becoming truly centred on the source of our life and being. It is an ongoing commitment to live a holy life, open to the promptings of the Spirit, willing to witness before all people to the truth of Jesus Christ.

The vow of hospitality means welcoming the 'other', opening forth a space wherein the other feels included and comfortable. It is so necessary in today's society of isolation and alienation to promote the values of Gospel living. Hospitality is crossing this threshold into a new way of living and being. The sacred aspect of crossing this threshold is reflected in allowing others to be their true selves.

The vow of obedience teaches us the importance of the 'other', learning to discern God's will in the hustle and bustle of everyday life. Through the practice of obedience we discover the authentic call to open into life-giving dialogue. This vow teaches us that we are part of a community – one where each member uniquely contributes to the well-being of the others through a life of service.

The vow of stability enables us to root ourselves in the person of Jesus Christ. We learn to live from Him and in Him. To have stability we must find equilibrium. This is reflected in the way we relate to the world and indeed, to each other, finding harmony in the structures of modern living – living within the tensions which surround us – acknowledging the primacy of Christ in our world.

Benedictine spirituality is, in short, a balanced way of life for people who long for intimacy with God and yet find themselves distracted and immersed in practical duties and problems. It is founded on silence, holy reading, prayer and work. It's an invitation to each of us to live our baptismal vocation within the heart of a community.

Anthony OSB

The seven sections of this book – whose language is non-inclusive at times and traditional in places – are loosely based on The Rule. Further information appears at the back, including the 1995 Church Survey (see p. 231). A detailed table of contents is also provided.

Rosemary C. Curtis
Summer 1997

1

THE FAMILY OF CHRIST

THEN I SAW another angel flying in mid-heaven, with an eternal gospel to proclaim to those who dwell on earth, to every nation and tribe and tongue and people; and he said with a loud voice, 'Fear God and give him glory, for the hour of his judgment has come; and worship him who made heaven and earth, the sea and the fountains of water.'

Revelation 14 v 6–7, RSV

E te whanau a te Karaiti,* Brothers and sisters in Christ, let us praise and worship God who has called us together.

Liturgies of the Word
A New Zealand Prayer Book[1]

*(pronounced Aye tay fanaaoo aaar tay Karaiti,)

REMEMBER, O Lord, your church.
Deliver it from evil and perfect it in your love.
Strengthen and preserve it by your word and
    sacraments.
Extend its influence,
that your gospel may be preached to all
    nations.
Gather the faithful from throughout the world
into the kingdom which you have prepared,
through Jesus Christ our Lord.

                                    Swedish Liturgy

A PUBLIC celebration is a rope-bridge of
knotted symbols strung across an abyss.
We make our crossings hoping the chasm
will echo our festive sounds for a moment, as
the bridge begins to sway from the rhythms of
our dance.

                                    Ronald Grimes

THE LIVING Christ still has two hands,
one to point the way,
and the other held out to help us along.

T. W. Mason

RELIGION is in the heart
Not in the knees.

Douglas Jerrold

Morning Prayer

The Collect

O LORD, OUR heavenly Father, Almighty and everlasting God, who hast safely brought us to the beginning of this day; Defend us in the same with thy mighty power; and grant that this day we fall into no sin, neither run into any kind of danger; but that all our doings may be ordered by thy governance, to do always what is righteous in thy sight; through Jesus Christ our Lord.

The Book of Common Prayer

I WAS GLAD when they said unto me: We will go into the house of the Lord.

Our feet shall stand in thy gates: O Jerusalem.

Jerusalem is built as a city: that is at unity in itself.

For thither the tribes go up, even the tribes of the Lord: to testify unto Israel, to give thanks unto the Name of the Lord.

For there is the seat of judgement: even the seat of the house of David.

O pray for the peace of Jerusalem: they shall prosper that love thee.

Peace be within thy walls: and plenteousness within thy palaces.

For my brethren and companions' sakes: I will wish thee prosperity.

Yea, because of the house of the Lord our God: I will seek to do thee good.

The Book of Common Prayer

EVERY MORNING put thy mind into thy heart
And stand in the presence of God all day long.

An Eastern monk

O WORSHIP the Lord in the beauty of holiness!
Bow down before him, his glory proclaim;
With gold of obedience, and incense of
   lowliness,
Kneel and adore him, the Lord is his name!

Low at his feet lay thy burden of carefulness,
High on his heart he will bear it for thee,
Comfort thy sorrows, and answer thy
   prayerfulness,
Guiding thy steps as may best for thee be.

Fear not to enter his courts in the slenderness
Of thy poor wealth thou wouldst reckon as thine:
Truth in its beauty, and love in its tenderness,
These are the offerings to lay on his shrine.

These, though we bring them in trembling and
   fearfulness,
He will accept for the name that is dear;
Mornings of joy give for evenings of
   tearfulness,
Trust for our trembling and hope for our fear.

O worship the Lord in the beauty of holiness!
Bow down before him, his glory proclaim;
With gold of obedience, and incense of
   lowliness,
Kneel and adore him, the Lord is his name!

J.S.B. Monsell

GIVE TO YOUR Church, O God,
a bold vision and a daring charity,
a refreshed wisdom and a courteous
    understanding,
that the eternal message of your Son
may be acclaimed as the good news of the
    age;
through him who makes all things new,
even Jesus Christ our Lord. Amen.

Celebrating Common Prayer

Mid-day Office

CHRIST JESUS, even if we had faith enough
to move mountains, without living charity,
what would we be?
    You love us.
Without your Holy Spirit who lives in our
hearts, what would we be?
    You love us.
Taking everything upon yourself, you open
for us a way towards faith, towards trust in
God, who wants neither suffering nor human
distress.
    Spirit of the Risen Christ, Spirit of com-
passion, Spirit of praise, your love for each
one of us will never disappear.

Prayer by Brother Roger of Taizé

I WILL LIFT UP mine eyes unto the hills: from whence cometh my help.

My help cometh even from the Lord: who hath made heaven and earth.

He will not suffer thy foot to be moved: and he that keepeth thee will not sleep.

The Lord himself is thy keeper: the Lord is thy defence upon thy right hand;

So that the sun shall not burn thee by day: neither the moon by night.

The Lord shall preserve thee from all evil: yea, it is even he that shall keep thy soul.

The Lord shall preserve thy going out, and thy coming in: from this time forth for evermore.

The Book of Common Prayer

A General Thanksgiving

ALMIGHTY GOD, Father of all mercies, We thine unworthy servants do give thee most humble and hearty thanks for all thy goodness and loving-kindness To us and to all men; We bless thee for our creation, preservation and all the blessings of this life; But above all for thy inestimable love In the redemption of the world by our Lord Jesus

Christ, For the means of grace, And for the hope of glory. And we beseech thee, give us that due sense of all thy mercies, That our hearts may be unfeignedly thankful, and that we shew forth thy praise, not only with our lips, but in our lives; By giving up ourselves to thy service, And by walking before thee in holiness and righteousness all our days; through Jesus Christ our Lord, to whom with thee and the Holy Ghost be all honour and glory, world without end. Amen.

The Book of Common Prayer

Completion of the Day

PRESERVE US, O Lord, while waking,
and guard us while sleeping,
that awake we may watch with Christ,
and asleep we may rest in peace.

Celebrating Common Prayer

Psalm 67

GOD BE MERCIFUL unto us, and bless us: and shew us the light of his countenance, and be merciful unto us:

That thy way may be known upon earth: thy saving health among all nations.

Let the people praise thee, O God: yea, let all the people praise thee.

O let the nations rejoice and be glad: for thou shalt judge the folk righteously, and govern the nations upon earth.

Let the people praise thee, O God: let all the people praise thee.

Then shall the earth bring forth her increase: and God, even our own God, shall give us his blessing.

God shall bless us: and all the ends of the world shall fear him.

The Book of Common Prayer

BE PRESENT, O merciful God
and protect me through the silent hours of this night,
so that I who am wearied by the changes
and chances of this fleeting world
may rest upon your eternal changelessness;
through Jesus Christ my Lord.

Celebrating Common Prayer

AT THIS HOUR, O Lord, some souls pass from this life into the unknown world. May their release be merciful, and may they find light in thee, who art the God of all flesh and the victor over the grave.

A Saint Francis Prayer Book

MAY THE SOULS of the faithful departed
Through the mercy of God
Rest in Peace
And rise in glory

The Sacraments[2]

DO NOT SUPPOSE that you can store grace within yourself, and carry on. It cannot be done. Grace flows like sunlight from God to us, and can no more be stored than sunlight can be stored. You must turn your face to the rays.

Austin Farrer (adapted)

Preparation for Holy Communion

WORSHIP GOD in a way that is worthy of thinking beings, by offering your living bodies as a holy sacrifice, truly pleasing to God.

Romans 12 v 1
The Daily Missal

IF YOU CAME this way,
Taking any route, starting from anywhere,
At any time or at any season,
It would always be the same: you would have
to put off
Sense and notion. You are not here to verify,
Instruct yourself, or inform curiosity
Or carry report. You are here to kneel
Where prayer has been valid. And prayer is more
Than an order of words, the conscious
occupation
Of the praying mind, or the sound of the voice
praying.
And what the dead had no speech for, when
living,
They can tell you, being dead: the
communication
Of the dead is tongued with fire beyond the
language of the living.
Here, the intersection of the timeless moment ...

T.S. Eliot

MOMENTS of great calm,
Kneeling before an altar
Of wood in a stone church
In summer, waiting for the God
To speak; the air a staircase
For silence; the sun's light
Ringing me, as though I acted
A great role. And the audiences
Still; all that close throng
Of spirits waiting, as I,
For the message.
Prompt me, God;
But not yet. When I speak
Though it be you who speak
Through me, something is lost.
The meaning is in the waiting.

R.S. Thomas

GO FORWARD, then, with simple, undoubting faith, and come to this Sacrament with humble reverence, confidently committing to Almighty God whatever you are not able to understand. God never deceives; but man is deceived whenever he puts too much trust in himself. God walks with the simple, reveals himself to the humble, gives understanding to little ones, discloses his secrets to pure minds, and conceals his grace from the curious and conceited. All reason and natural research must follow faith, but not precede or encroach on it. For in this most holy and excellent Sacrament faith and love precede all else, working in ways unknowable to man. The eternal God, transcendent and infinite in power, works mightily and unsearchably both in heaven and earth, nor can there be any searching out of his wonders. For were the works of God readily understandable by human reason, they would be neither wonderful nor unspeakable.

Thomas à Kempis

Holy Communion

FOR THE BREAD that we have eaten
For the wine that we have tasted
For the life that you have given:
Father, Son and Holy Spirit,
We will praise you.

For the life of Christ within us
Turning all our fears to freedom
Helping us to live for others:
Father, Son and Holy Spirit,
We will praise you.

15

For the strength of Christ to lead us
In our living and our dying,
In the end with all your people
Father, Son and Holy Spirit,
We will praise you.

Contemporary Prayers for
Public Worship

ALMIGHTY GOD, we thank you for feeding us with the body and blood of your Son Jesus Christ. Through him we offer you our souls and bodies to be a living sacrifice. Send us out in the power of your Spirit to live and work to your praise and glory.

Go in peace to love and serve the Lord. In the name of Christ.

The Alternative Service Book

The Incarnation

Angelus

THE ANGEL of the Lord brought tidings to Mary
And she conceived by the Holy Spirit.

Hail Mary, full of grace, the Lord is with you.
Blessed are you among women,

16

and blessed is the fruit of your womb, Jesus.
Holy Mary, Mother of God, pray for us sinners,
now, and at the hour of our death.

'Behold, the handmaid of the Lord;
Let it be to me according to your word.'

Hail Mary ...

The Word was made flesh
And dwelt among us.

Hail Mary ...

Pray for us, O holy Mother of God,
That we may be made worthy of the promises
    of Christ.

Let us pray.

We beseech you, O Lord,
to pour your grace into our hearts;
that as we have known the incarnation
of your Son Jesus Christ
by the message of an angel,
so by his cross and passion
we may be brought to the glory of his
    resurrection;
through Jesus Christ our Lord.

Celebrating Common Prayer

The Birth of a Child

HEAVENLY FATHER, creator and giver of life, there is such joy in our hearts at the news of a baby's birth, a most special and complete gift of your love, a new being and a wonder of creation.

Be with the mother and father of this little baby in their happiness, and accept their praise and ours as we give thanks to you, through Jesus Christ our Lord.

Mothers' Union

Baptism

WE RECEIVE this child into the Congregation of Christ's flock, and do sign him with the sign of the Cross, in token that hereafter he shall not be ashamed to confess the faith of Christ crucified, and manfully to fight under his banner against sin, the world, and the devil, and to continue Christ's faithful soldier and servant unto his life's end.

The Book of Common Prayer

Confirmation

Defend, O Lord, this thy Child with thy heavenly grace, that he may continue thine for ever; and daily increase in thy Holy Spirit, more and more, until he come unto thy everlasting kingdom.

The Book of Common Prayer

For Vocations

Almighty God, you have entrusted to your Church a share in the ministry of your Son, our great High Priest. Inspire by your Holy Spirit the hearts and minds of many to offer themselves for the sacred ministry, that as deacons and priests they may draw all men to your kingdom; through Jesus Christ our Lord.

The Alternative Service Book

The end of all things is upon us, so you must lead an ordered and sober life, given to prayer. Above all, keep your love for one another at full strength, because love cancels innumerable sins. Be hospitable to one

19

another without complaining. Whatever gift each of you may have received, use it in service to one another, like good stewards dispensing the grace of God in its varied forms. Are you a speaker? Speak as if you uttered oracles of God. Do you give service? Give it as in the strength which God supplies. In all things so act that the glory may be God's through Jesus Christ; to him belong glory and power for ever and ever.

1 Peter 4 v 7–11, NEB

For those to be Ordained

ALMIGHTY GOD, giver of all good gifts, by your Holy Spirit you have appointed various orders of ministry in the Church. Look with mercy and favour on your servants now called to be deacons and priests. Maintain them in truth and renew them in holiness, that by word and good example they may faithfully serve you to the glory of your name and the benefit of your Church; through the merits of our Saviour Jesus Christ.

Ministers of the Church

GRANT, O GOD, we beseech thee, that the same mind may be in all the ministers of thy Church that was in Christ Jesus:
   his self-forgetting humility;
   his interest in common things;
   his love for common people;
   his compassion for the fallen;
   his tolerance with the mistaken;
   his patience with the slow;
and in all their work and converse make them continually sensitive to thy guidance and ready for thy will; through Jesus Christ our Lord.

Methodist Book of Offices

Marriage

FORASMUCH AS N. and N. have consented together in holy wedlock, and have witnessed the same before God and this company, and thereto have given and pledged their troth either to other, and have declared the same by giving and receiving of a ring, and by joining of hands; I pronounce that they may be man and wife together, In the

Name of the Father, and of the Son, and of
the Holy Ghost.

The Book of Common Prayer

Seasons of the Church's Year: Advent

LORD OUR GOD,
help us to prepare
for the coming of Christ, your Son.
May he find us waiting,
eager in joyful prayer.

The Daily Missal

Advent Preface

AND NOW WE give you thanks because you
prepared the way of your Son Jesus Christ
by the preaching of your servant John the
Baptist, who proclaimed him as the Lamb of
God, our Saviour.

The Alternative Service Book

CHRISTMAS is really
for the children.
Especially for children
who like animals, stables,
stars and babies wrapped
in swaddling clothes.
Then there are wise men,
kings in fine robes,
humble shepherds and a
hint of rich perfume.

Easter is not really
for children
unless accompanied by a
cream filled egg.
It has whips, blood, nails,
a spear and allegations
of body snatching.
It involves politics, God
and the sins of the world.
It is not good for people
of a nervous disposition.
They would do better to
think on rabbits, chickens
and the first snowdrop
of spring.
Or they'd do better to
wait for a re-run of
Christmas without asking

too many questions about
what Jesus did when he grew up
or whether there's any connection.

Steve Turner

THEN HEROD called the Magi secretly and found out from them the exact time the star had appeared. He sent them to Bethlehem and said, 'Go and make a careful search for the child. As soon as you find him, report to me, so that I too may go and worship him.' And having been warned in a dream not to go back to Herod, they returned to their country by another route.

Matthew 2 v 7,8,12, NIV

THERE ARE PEOPLE after Jesus.
They have seen the signs.
Quick, let's hide him.

Let's think: carpenter,
fisherman's friend,
disturber of religious comfort.
Let's award him a degree in theology,
a purple cassock
and a position of respect.
They'll never think of looking there.

Let's think: his dialect may betray him,
his tongue is of the masses.
Let's teach him Latin
and seventeenth century English.
They'll never think of listening in.

Let's think: humble,
Man of Sorrows,
nowhere to lay his head.
We'll build a house for him,
somewhere away from the poor.
We'll fill it with brass and silence.
It's sure to throw them off.

There are people after Jesus.
Quick, let's hide him.

Steve Turner

Advent Blessing

CHRIST THE SUN of Righteousness shine
upon you and scatter the darkness from
before your path; and the blessing of God
Almighty, the Father, the Son, and the Holy
Spirit, be among, and remain with you
always.

The Alternative Service Book

INTO THIS HOLY place at this happy time, O Lord, we come to worship that little child whose nature revealed thine own and what ours might become. We ask that the lovely things in his nature may grow in us and that all things hostile to his spirit may die. For his name's sake.

Leslie D. Weatherhead

MAY THE JOY of the angels,
the eagerness of the shepherds,
the perseverance of the wise men,
the obedience of Joseph and Mary,
and the peace of the Christ child
be yours this Christmas.
And the blessing of God Almighty, the Father, the Son and the Holy Spirit, be upon you and remain with you always.

The Promise of His Glory

GOD OF LOVE, open the hearts and minds of many this Christmas time to the good and saving news of Jesus Christ; that those whose lives are insecure, or empty, or aimless, may find in the one born at

Bethlehem all that they need today, and much more besides. For his name's sake.

Worship Now

AMONG THE OXEN (like an ox I'm slow)
I see a glory in the stable grow
Which, with the ox's dullness might at length
Give me an ox's strength.

Among the asses (stubborn I as they)
I see my Saviour where I looked for hay;
So may my beastlike folly learn at least
The patience of a beast.

Among the sheep (I like a sheep have strayed)
I watch the manger where my Lord is laid;
Oh that my baa-ing nature would win thence
Some woolly innocence!

C.S. Lewis

Epiphany

The Collect

ETERNAL GOD,
who by the shining of a star
led the wise men to the worship of your Son:

guide by his light the nations of the earth,
that the whole world may behold your glory;
through Jesus Christ our Lord.

The Alternative Service Book

WISE MEN seeking Jesus
Travelled from afar,
Guided on their journey
By a beauteous star.

But if we desire him,
He is close at hand;
For our native country
Is our Holy Land.

Prayerful souls may find him
By our quiet lakes,
Meet him on the hillsides
When the morning breaks.

In our fertile cornfields
While the sheaves are bound
In our busy markets,
Jesus may be found.

Fishermen talk with him
By the great North Sea,
As the disciples
Did in Galilee.

Every peaceful village
In our land might be
Made by Jesu's presence
Like sweet Bethany.

He is more than near us,
If we love him well;
For he seeketh ever
In our hearts to dwell.

James Thomas East

O GOD, OUR FATHER, Creator of the universe, whose Son, Jesus Christ, came to our world, pour your Holy Spirit upon your Church, that all the people of the world, being led through the knowledge of your truth to worship you, may offer the gold of intellect, the frankincense of devotion and the myrrh of discipline to him who is with you and the Holy Spirit who liveth and reigneth forever one God, world without end.

Church of Ceylon (Sri Lanka)

LORD JESUS, may your light shine upon our way,
as once it guided the steps of the magi:
that we too may be led into your presence
and worship you,

the Child of Mary
the Word of the Father,
the King of nations,
the Saviour of mankind;
to whom glory for ever.

Frank Colquhoun

Candlemas

*(The Presentation of Christ in the Temple –
2 February)*

This is a feast rich in meaning, with several related themes running through it – presentation, purification, meeting, light for the world. The several names by which it has been known in Christian history illustrate just how much it has to teach and to celebrate.

The Procession with lighted candles is the distinctive feature of the Eucharist of Candlemas, when *Nunc Dimittis* is sung.

Dear friends: Forty days ago we celebrated the birth of our Lord Jesus Christ. Now we recall the day on which he was presented in the Temple, when he was offered to the Father and shown to his people. As a sign

30

of his coming among us, his mother was purified, as we now come to him for cleansing. In their old age Simeon and Anna recognised him as their Lord, as we today sing of his glory. In this eucharist, we celebrate both the joy of his coming and his searching judgement, looking back to the day of his birth and forward to the coming days of his passion.

Lord, now lettest thou thy servant depart in peace:
according to thy word.

For mine eyes have seen thy salvation:
which thou hast prepared before the face of all people;

To be a light to lighten the Gentiles:
and to be the glory of thy people Israel.

Glory be to the Father, and to the Son, and to the Holy Ghost:
as it was in the beginning, is now, and ever shall be, world without end.

The Promise of His Glory

GRANT, WE BESEECH thee, O Lord, that by the observance of this Lent we may advance in the knowledge of the mystery of Christ, and show forth his mind in conduct worthy of our calling; through Jesus Christ our Lord.

Gelasian Sacramentary

The Collect for the Second Sunday in Lent

ALMIGHTY GOD, who seest that we have no power of ourselves to help ourselves: keep us both outwardly in our bodies, and inwardly in our souls; that we may be defended from all adversities which may happen to the body, and from all evil thoughts which may assault and hurt the soul; through Jesus Christ our Lord. Amen.

The Book of Common Prayer

LORD,
during this lenten season
nourish us with your word of life
and make us one in love and prayer.

The Daily Missal

MERCIFUL FATHER,
may the penance of our lenten observance
make us your obedient people.
May the love within us be seen in what we
    do
and lead us to the joy of Easter.

The Daily Missal

Mothering Sunday

MOTHERHOOD was never easy,
not for Mary, not for us.
There's longing in it, waiting, pain,
hard work and tight budgets.
But you, creating God, come that way,
lighting with glory the bond of trust
        and humble devotion.
Speak to us, God, through our mothers
        that we may know your steadfast love.

Bernard Thorogood

Palm Sunday

AS ON THIS DAY we keep the special memory of our redeemer's entry into the city, so grant, O Lord, that now and ever he may triumph in our hearts. Let the king of grace and glory enter in, and let us lay ourselves and all we are in full joyful homage before him; through the same Jesus Christ our Lord.

Handley C. G. Moule

Easter

The Easter Triduum

LENT LASTS UNTIL the Evening of Maundy Thursday. The Mass of the Last Supper until the Evening Prayer of Easter Sunday inclusively constitutes the Easter Triduum, which is of even greater antiquity than the Season of Lent.

The Lectionary

LORD JESUS CHRIST, who when thou wast able to institute thy holy sacrament at the Last Supper, didst wash the feet of the apostles, and teach us by thy example the grace of humility: cleanse us, we beseech thee, from all stain of sin, that we may be worthy partakers of thy holy mysteries; who livest and reignest with the Father and the Holy Ghost, one God, world without end.

Church of England (Office of the Royal Maundy in Westminster Abbey)

FROM THE FOOT of the cross I look up to thee
O Jesus Lord bow down to me.
For I stand in the faith of my God today
Put love in my heart and hope alway.

Source Unknown (early Scottish)

THOU WHOSE ETERNAL love for our weak and struggling race was most perfectly shown forth in the blessed life and death of Jesus Christ our Lord, enable me now so to meditate upon my Lord's passion that, having fellowship with him in sorrow, I may also learn the secret of his strength and peace.

John Baillie

FAR FROM MY PARISH on the Monday afternoon of Holy Week, 1995, I slipped into a familiar church for some solitary reflection after an arduous 'journey'.

Standing beneath the Rose Window, the holiness and quiet engulfed me. Slowly — very slowly — my thoughts went back 2,000 years ...

From my distant position in the church, the linen made sombre viewing: a stark, cruel, black, Crown of Thorns. It demanded scrutiny, and I moved towards it.

Standing beneath the pulpit, inches from the linen, the stitches were not black at all. The embroiderer's eyes had yanked from a hedge a dreadfully thorny, decayed, brown stem and then had skilfully fashioned awesome stitches into bleak reality. The event, and the artist's work, pierced the viewer to the full ...

But, seen contemplatively, there was the actual, certain, hope of the Resurrection: on each of the tiniest end-tips of the cruellest crown of all, were the minutest stitches of — **GREEN!**

R.C.C.

The Vigil

BROTHERS AND SISTERS in Christ, on this most holy night, in which our Lord Jesus Christ passed over from death to life, the Church invites her members, dispersed throughout the world, to gather in vigil and prayer. For this is the Passover of the Lord, in which through word and sacrament we share in his victory over death.

As we await the risen Christ, let us hear the record of God's saving deeds in history, recalling how he saved his people in ages past and in the fullness of time sent his Son to be our Redeemer; and let us pray that through this Easter celebration God may bring to perfection in each of us the saving work he has begun.

The Renewal of Baptismal Vows

AS WE CELEBRATE the resurrection of our Lord Jesus Christ from the dead, we remember that through the paschal mystery we have died and been buried with him in baptism, so that we may rise with him to a new life within the family of his Church. Now that we have completed our observance of Lent, we renew the promises made at our baptism, affirming our allegiance to Christ, and our rejection of all that is evil.

Lent, Holy Week and Easter

Easter Day

JESUS CHRIST is risen today,   Alleluia.
our triumphant holy day,   Alleluia.
who did once, upon the cross, Alleluia.
suffer to redeem our loss.   Alleluia.

Hymns of praise then let us sing
unto Christ, our heavenly King,
who endured the cross and grave,
sinners to redeem and save.

But the pains that he endured
our salvation hath procured;
now above the sky he's King,
where the angels ever sing.

Hymns A & M New Standard

Ascension Day

The Preface

FATHER, all-powerful and ever-living God,
we do well always and everywhere to give
you thanks,

(Today) the Lord Jesus, the king of glory,
the conqueror of sin and death,
ascended to heaven while the angels sang
his praises.

Christ, the mediator between God and man,
judge of the world and Lord of all,
has passed beyond our sight,
not to abandon us but to be our hope.
Christ is the beginning, the head
of the Church;
where he has gone, we hope to follow.

The joy of the resurrection and ascension
renews the whole world, while the choirs of
heaven sing for ever to your glory;
Holy, Holy, Holy Lord, God of power and might.
Heaven and earth are full of your glory.
Hosanna in the highest.
Blessed is he who comes in the name of the
Lord
Hosanna in the highest.

The Sunday Missal

The Holy Spirit

Pentecost: The Preface

FATHER, all-powerful and ever-living God,
we do well always and everywhere to give
you thanks.

Today you sent the Holy Spirit
on those marked out to be your children
by sharing the life of your only Son,
and so you brought the paschal mystery to
its completion.

Today we celebrate the great beginning of
your Church
when the Holy Spirit made known to all
peoples the one true God,
and created from the many languages of man
one voice to profess one faith.

The joy of the resurrection renews the whole
world,
while the choirs of heaven sing for ever to
your glory:
Holy, holy, holy Lord, God of power and
might.
Heaven and earth are full of your glory.
Hosanna in the highest.

Blessed is he who comes in the name of the
Lord
Hosanna in the highest.

The Sunday Missal

COMPANIONS let us pray together,
in this place affirm our faith.
God who made us is here among us,
we stand together in God's grace.

We are whanau [family] we are one,
brothers, sisters of the Son.
We are reaching for our freedom,
the prize that Christ has won.

The broken Christ stands here among us,
shares our suffering and our pain.
In breaking bread we find empowerment
to live in aroha [love] again.

The risen Christ brings light and laughter,
celebrates the life we share.
The poured out wine of Christ's self-giving
inspires us to reach out and care.

Now let us sing to God who loves us
and accepts us as we are.
Go out from here and live the message,
proclaim our oneness near and far.

David Clark and Witi Ihimaera

MY GOD, GRANT ME the conversion of the parish; I am willing to suffer all my life whatsoever please thee to lay upon me; yes even for a hundred years am I prepared to endure the sharpest pains, only let the people be converted. My God, convert the parish.

Curé d'Ars (adapted)

Corpus Christi

Thanksgiving for the Institution of Holy Communion

ALMIGHTY and heavenly Father,
we thank you that in this wonderful
   sacrament
you have given us the memorial
of the passion of your Son Jesus Christ.
Grant us so to reverence
the sacred mysteries of his body and blood,
that we may know within ourselves
and show forth in our lives the fruits of his
   redemption;
who is alive and reigns with you and the
   Holy Spirit,
one God, now and for ever.

The Alternative Service Book

All Saints' Day

O ALMIGHTY GOD, who hast knit together thine elect in one communion and fellowship, in the mystical body of thy Son Christ our Lord: Grant us grace so to follow thy blessed Saints in all virtuous and godly living, that we may come to those unspeakable joys, which thou hast prepared for them that unfeignedly love thee; through Jesus Christ our Lord.

The Book of Common Prayer

FOR ALL THE SAINTS who from their labours
   rest,
Who thee by faith before the world
   confessed,
Thy name, O Jesu, be for ever blest. Alleluia!

Thou wast their rock, their fortress, and their
   might;
Thou, Lord, their captain in the well-fought
   fight;
Thou, in the darkness drear their one true
   light. Alleluia!

O may thy soldiers, faithful, true and bold,
Fight as the saints who nobly fought of old,
And win, with them, the victor's crown of
   gold. Alleluia!

O blest communion! fellowship divine!
We feebly struggle, they in glory shine;
Yet all are one in thee, for all are thine.
  Alleluia!

But lo! there breaks a yet more glorious day;
The saints in triumph rise in bright array;
The King of glory passes on his way. Alleluia!

From earth's wide bounds, from ocean's
  farthest coast,
Through gates of pearl streams in the
  countless host,
Singing to Father, Son, and Holy Ghost.
  Alleluia!

Richard Mant

ALMIGHTY AND ever-living God, we offer thee most hearty thanks for the grace and virtue made manifest in all thy saints, who have been chosen vessels of thy favour and lights of the world in their several generations: and we most humbly beseech thee to give us grace so to follow their good examples that with them we may be partakers of thy heavenly kingdom; through Jesus Christ our Lord.

Methodist Church Book of Offices

All Souls' Day

O ALMIGHTY GOD, the God of the spirits of all flesh: Multiply, we beseech thee, to those who rest in Jesus, the manifold blessings of thy love, that the good work which thou didst begin in them may be perfected unto the day of Jesus Christ. And of thy mercy, O heavenly Father, vouchsafe that we who now serve thee here on earth, may, at the last, together with them, be found meet to be partakers of the inheritance of the saints in light; for the sake of the same thy Son Jesus Christ our Lord and Saviour.

Scottish Prayer Book

Remembrance Sunday

LET US remember before God,
and commend to his sure keeping:
  those who have died for their country in war;
  those whom we knew, and whose memory
  we treasure;
  and all who have lived and died
  in the service of mankind.

They shall grow not old as we that are left
  grow old:

Age shall not weary them, nor the years
   condemn.
At the going down of the sun and in the
   morning
We will remember them.

The Promise of His Glory

Prayer for Choristers

BLESS, O LORD, your servants who minister
in your temple. Grant that what we sing with
our lips we may believe in our hearts, and
that what we believe in our hearts we may
show forth in our lives. Through Jesus Christ
our Lord.

The Royal School of Church Music

Music

O GOD our Father, we thank you for the joy
of music. We also thank you for composers
and performers who, through their gifts and
dedication, enable you to reach souls. We
rejoice in our senses, and how music can

unite people and nations and can, also, inspire, comfort, revive memories and release emotions.

R.C.C.

Prayer for Churchworkers

ALMIGHTY FATHER, from whom every family in heaven and earth is named, who has called us into the fellowship of thy church; grant we beseech thee, that in all our parishes and circuits we may fulfil the duties and enjoy the privileges of our spiritual home. And upon those who offer themselves for thy service bestow the fulness of thy grace; that united in love to thee and to one another, we may show forth thy glory and hasten the coming of thy kingdom.

Source Unknown (adapted)

2

PRIVATE PRAYER

The Value of Prayer

MY SPIRIT is dry within me because it forgets
to feed on thee

> John of the Cross

IF WE RELY ON the outward observances of
religion, our devotion will rapidly wane.

> Thomas à Kempis

GIVE US O GOD:
Thoughts which turn into prayer,
Love which turns into deeds.

> Ronald H. Lloyd

ACTION SHOULD be something added to the
life of prayer, not something taken away
from it.

> St Thomas Aquinas

THEN SAID Evangelist,
Pointing with his finger
Over a very wide field,
Do you see yonder wicket-gate?
The man said, No.
Then said Evangelist,
Do you see yonder
Shining light?

He said, I think I do.
Then said Evangelist,
Keep that light in your eye.

Pilgrim's Progress

EVERY TIME I see a church
I always go and visit.
So when at last I'm carried in
The Lord won't say:
'Who is it?'

Note found pinned in the porch
of Old Romney Church

BEGIN THEN TO PRAISE [pray] now, if thou intendest to praise for ever ... Praise and bless the Lord thy God every single day, so that when the time of single days has passed, and there has come that one day without end, thou mayest go from praise to praise, as from strength to strength.

St Augustine

HE PRAYETH WELL, who loveth well
Both man and bird and beast.

He prayeth best, who loveth best
All things both great and small;

For the dear God who loveth us,
He made and loveth all.

Samuel Taylor Coleridge

NO, IT IS NOT so much what we 'do' or try to do that is important, but what we are. 'Being' rather than 'doing' comes first, for what we do comes out of what we are.

Sister Agnes SOLI

The Art of Prayer

LORD, I AM STIFF and rigid in my prayers. I need to loosen up. To talk to you as a human being. To discuss my problems and my fears with you. To behave as a disciple and not as a distant admirer, setting you on a pedestal where I feel sure you have no desire to be. I would like very much to enjoy my prayers. To feel as relaxed as I do when taking a walk in the country. I would like to enjoy my communion with you as much as I enjoy a piece of good music or a good ballet. I must make my mind work at my prayer so that I can bring everything into it. I know you are interested. It is I who am dull and stiff and 'mannered'. Humanize me, Lord.

Norman Goodacre

FROM THE COWARDICE that dare not face new truth,

from the laziness that is content with half truth,

from the arrogance that thinks it knows all truth,

Good Lord, deliver me.

Kenyan Prayer

LORD ...

My soul is so dry that by itself it cannot pray;
Yet you can squeeze from it the juice of a thousand prayers.

My soul is so parched that by itself it cannot love;
Yet you can draw from it boundless love for you and for my neighbour.

My soul is so cold that by itself it has no joy;
Yet you can light the fire of heavenly joy within me.

My soul is so feeble that by itself it has no faith;
Yet by your power my faith grows to a great height.

Thank you for prayer, for love, for joy, for faith;
Let me be always prayerful, loving, joyful and faithful.

Guido the Carthusian

Silence

WE NEED TO find God, and he cannot be found in noise and restlessness. God is the friend of silence. See how nature – trees, flowers, grass – grow in silence; see the stars, the moon and sun, how they move in silence. Is not our mission to give God to the poor in the slums? Not a dead God, but a living, loving God. The more we receive in silent prayer, the more we can give in our active life. We need silence to be able to touch souls. The essential thing is not what we say, but what God says to us and through us. All our words will be useless unless they come from within – words which do not give the light of Christ increase the darkness.

Mother Teresa

O LORD, THE SCRIPTURE says: 'There is a time for silence and a time for speech'. Saviour, teach me the silence of humility, the silence of wisdom, the silence of love, the silence of perfection, the silence that speaks without words, the silence of faith.

Lord, teach me to silence my own heart that I may listen to the gentle movement of the Holy Spirit within me and sense the depths which are of God.

Frankfurt prayer

Silence Alive

Silent Father
Silent Son
Silent Holy Spirit
Silent One – I love you.
In the silence of eyes
          I see you.
In the silence of unspoken words
          I hear you.
In the silence of sudden touch
          I feel you.
In the silence of a flower's fragrance
          I smell you.
In the silence of bread and wine
          I taste you.
Sensual God, I love you!
I love you in the silence –
          Silent Father
          Silent Son
          Silent Holy Spirit
          Silent One – I love you!

Harry Alfred Wiggett

PRAYER IS like watching for the
Kingfisher. All you can do is
Be where he is likely to appear, and
Wait.
Often, nothing much happens;
There is space, silence and
Expectancy.
No visible sign, only the
Knowledge that he's been there
And may come again.
Seeing or not seeing cease to matter,
You have been prepared.
But when you've almost stopped
Expecting it, a flash of brightness
Gives encouragement.

Ann Lewin

Listening to God

PRAYER IS relationship with God. Such
relationships presuppose communication
from both sides. Not only does a person
pray to God in words or unspoken thoughts,
but also God communicates with the praying
one in intuitions, often so clear that they can
be interpreted into direct speech. At such

times God's initiative is clearly apparent, and the heart is moved to respond in prayer or silent worship, or in inspired and obedient word or action.

George Appleton

Praise

O GOD, MY GOD
I praise you now for your hand on all my life:
for my conception and safe birth;
for my nurturing through childhood;
for education and leisure skills;
for tenderness and love in my family and beyond.

For my dreams of what my life might be;
for this civilisation in which I live, and my civil rights within it;
for such gifts of mind and person as I have, and some opportunities to use them.

For the work I have been able to do, and your sustaining in its heaviness and toil;
for your presence with me in unemployment, sustaining me in its emptiness and rejection.

For the times when money has been short, and you have met my need;
for the times when my income has been high, and you have taught me generosity and stewardship.

For love in relationships, and for the wonder of mutual commitment;
for the mysterious gift of marriage: the hopefulness of homemaking, the joys of physical intimacy, the slow learning of self-sacrifice and the glory of faithfulness.

For children, the wonder and joy of them, and all the fears and hopes for them;
for the renewing gift of their love, and your comfort when that disappoints.

For the companionship of friends, its tenderness and depth;
for comfort in desolate bereavement.

For the pleasure of health and energy, and the care of doctors and nurses when they fail.

For your beautiful world, with its creatures, and the challenge to conserve it and them.

For fair cities and strange peoples and the richness in learning of them.

For all simple joys; all gentle thoughts; all music, books, films and art which feed the mind and nourish the soul.

For your church, in its many forms; for all who truly worship
the one true God.

For the experience of the love of Christ in my life; for the joy of all who know him.

For the experience of eternal things in this life, and the hope of heaven hereafter.

O God, my God, how shall I thank you? With all my heart?
Yes, Lord.

Ruth Etchells (adapted)

The Written Word

FATHER, WE thank you for the gift of language and for the printed page.

We thank you for the books that have helped to shape our lives and to mould our tastes and values; that have furnished our minds, spoken to our hearts, enriched or entertained us, both in health and sickness.

Teach us to value the written word and to use it rightly; through him whose words are words of life, our Saviour Jesus Christ.

Frank Colquhoun

Confession

O THOU GREAT CHIEF, light a candle in my heart, that I may see what is therein, and sweep the rubbish from thy dwelling-place.

An African schoolgirl's prayer

LORD, YOU HAVE an enormous file on me. Your informers report all my movements, and you know what armchair, what theatre seat, what office stool I sit on, how I respond to my alarm clock and early cup of tea, the path I follow to factory, swimming pool, or church. You even have bugging devices to record my thoughts. You have photostats of all my air tickets, expense accounts, and hotel bookings. You have on tape everything I say in public and in private. You created me and you sustain me to the last detail.

Leslie Stradling

O LORD JESUS, we confess how quickly we see other people's faults, and how slow we are to recognise our own. Forgive us, and make us more forgiving; through Jesus Christ our Lord.

Beryl Bye

Forms of Self Examination

1 Corinthians 13 v 4–7: Love is ... Am I?
LOVE IS PATIENT.
Love is kind.
Love envies no-one.
Love is never boastful or conceited.
Love is not rude.
Love is never selfish.

Love is not quick to take offence.
Love keeps no score of wrongs.
Love does not gloat over other people's sins, but delights in the truth.
Ask each time: when am I not patient, kind: when am I envious, etc., and think of what person or situation makes you so. Only Jesus himself can answer all these in the affirmative, but our aim is to attain the measure of the stature of the fullness of Christ.

THE FRUIT of the Spirit is:
love, joy, peace, patience, kindness, goodness, faithfulness, gentleness, self-control: against these there is no law.
Ask: when am I not loving, joyous, peaceful, etc.? The persons and occasions that make me less than loving, joyous, peaceful, etc., point to the growing edge in my life as a Christian.

Brother Thomas Anthony SSF (adapted)

YOU GIVE ALL your sins to Jesus Christ and he pours on you all the blessings of the redemption.

Michel Quoist

LORD JESUS CHRIST, Son of God, have mercy upon me, a sinner.

Source Unknown

O LORD, FORGIVE what I have been, sanctify what I am, and order what I shall be.

Source Unknown

A CHILD asked me:
'What's this paper for?'
'For you to tell God
what you're sorry about,'
I replied, adding
'You can write it or draw.'
'I'll do both,' she said
and, borrowing my pen,
quickly drew a figure
and began to write.
'How do you spell people?'
she asked me –
direct and matter of fact
as if writing to God
was a daily task

hindered only by spelling.
Her question answered
she placed the folded paper
in the basket
with all the others.

Dear God,
I'm sorry.
Help me love people.

Janet Lees

Anima Christi

SOUL OF CHRIST sanctify me!
Body of Christ save me!
Blood of Christ refresh me!
Water from the side of Christ wash me!
Passion of Christ strengthen me!
O good Jesus hear me!
Within thy wounds hide me!
Suffer me not to be separated from Thee!
From the malicious enemy defend me!
In the hour of my death call me,
And bid me come to Thee;
That with thy saints I may praise Thee for
   all eternity.
May the Lord grant us His peace and life
   eternal.

Pope John XXII

Prayers for Children

O GOD, when we look about us for evidence
of your presence, open our minds so that we
may see you in:
the Geometry of the rainbow;
the Arithmetic of gravity;
the Physics of the thunder cloud;
the Chemistry of a raindrop;
the Engineering of a cobweb;
the Navigation of migratory birds.
We ask this in the name of Jesus Christ our
Lord.

Ronald H. Lloyd

MY MOTHER'S NAME is worry
In summer, my mother worries about water,
In winter, she worries about coal briquettes,
And all year long, she worries about rice.

In daytime, my mother worries about living,
At night, she worries for children.
And all day long, she worries and worries.

Then my mother's name is worry,
My father's is drunken frenzy,
And mine is tears and sighs.

A twelve-year-old child
in a slum area of Asia

DEAREST FATHER who lives in heaven,
may your name be kept pure.
Let peace reign and let everyone be equal
on earth as well as in heaven.
Provide us with our daily needs as well as
our spiritual needs.
Please forgive us the things we have done
wrong
as we will forget the bad things others have
done to us.
Help us not to be tempted to hurt you
and keep Satan away from us.
Because you made the earth and heaven
and everything in it
and you are all powerful and we should give
you glory
through all eternity.
We all agree with this!

Children's Camp, North India
(aged eight to fourteen)

The Home

LORD, BLESS THIS HOUSE and all who live in it.
Hallow it with your presence and your peace.
Let it be a place where prayer is made,
where love abounds,

where your name is honoured;
and may your fatherly hand be over us day
   by day,
in our going out and coming in,
now and for evermore.

Frank Colquhoun

LET US ASK GOD to bless our home.
Jesus, King of love, you shared in the life of
your earthly home at Nazareth with Mary
and Joseph. Bless, we pray, our new home
and our life here, that we may help each
other and those who visit us to grow more
and more in your love. We ask this in your
name and for your sake.

The Alternative Service Book
Anglican Church of Canada

BLESS OUR HOME, Father,
that we cherish the bread
before there is none,
discover each other
before we leave,
and enjoy each other
for what we are
while we have time.

Author Unknown

Parents, teachers and children

CREATOR GOD, life is sacred and time is sacramental. Guide and direct all those at home or in schools who have the priceless delight of a child's upbringing and education. May love and discipline be well-mixed and sacrifices cheerfully made. Pour your blessings on all children, parents and teachers. In the west we may not always achieve the ideals we seek, but we can be grateful that in so many parts of the world our homelife and education can be the envy of millions.

R.C.C.

Praying for Other People

NEVER SAY, Can I move God by my prayers? But always reflect: The blessings of God are piling against my door. Up, open and let in the avalanche of gold. Some will remain in my house with me, some will pass on through me to other hands. Ah, no, the division is false: no blessings so securely remain as those which pass on, for how can I be more blessed myself than in blessing my friends out of the heart and mouth of God?

Austin Farrer

ENFORCED separations are an anguish in our hearts, but in offering them first to you, we truly love. Eternal God, we offer to you all those we love, and miss most. Bless them with health, happiness and safety and that wherever they are we are united with them, in you.

R.C.C.

MY FATHER in heaven, I remember those whom in prayer I am inclined to forget.
I pray for those whom I dislike.
Defend me against my own feelings;
change my inclinations;
give me a compassionate heart.
Give me, I pray, the purity of heart
which finds your image in all people.

J. H. Jowett

The Lonely

GENTLE loving Lord, be with those today
   (tonight) who are alone and have no one to
   pray for them:
No one who shares and cares,
No one to hold their hands,
No one who smiles with them,
No one to give most basic care.
In their Gethsemane today (tonight) banish
   their loneliness.

R.C.C.

LORD, GRANT ME the gift of seeing others as
   persons – not just as male or female, child
   or grown-up, black or white, rich or poor.
Let me see their hearts, so that they can
   inspire me.
Let me see their needs, so that I can help
   them.
Let me see their gifts, so that they can help
   me.
Let me see their sorrows, so that I can
   comfort them.
Let me see their joys, so that I can share
   them.
Let me see their wisdom, so that I can learn
   from them.

Let me see their love, and make us friends.
And use us to fulfil your purpose for your
   people.
In the name of our Lord Jesus Christ.

A Closer Walk With God

WE BRING to you in our prayers, heavenly
Father, all lonely people, especially those
who are too old or infirm to enjoy company,
and those who are isolated from others
through suffering and pain or through a
sense of inferiority. We pray that friends
or neighbours may be enabled to reach
them and lift them out of their loneliness
and bring them comfort and hope. We ask it
in Christ's name.

New Every Morning

WHAT CAN I bring to you, my Lord?
Bring what you have seen, my Son.

I have seen a child without hope
Bring all that to me

I have seen a man standing all alone
Bring all that to me

I have seen a woman mourn her son
Bring all that to me.

O Lord send your Holy Spirit on these
  gifts
Make them holy and become for us,
Jesus's Body and Blood
Their heavenly food
You gave us.

What can I bring to you my Lord?
Bring what you have heard.

I have heard the poor man's dying cry
Bring all that to me.

I have heard the word of peace denied
Bring all that to me

I have heard the word of love denied
Bring all that to me

Chorus
O Lord send your Holy Spirit on these
  gifts
Make them holy and become for us,
Jesus's Body and Blood
Their heavenly food
You gave us.

A prayer from the Sudan

Praying for Ourselves

BLESS TO ME, O God, the earth beneath my
 feet,
Bless to me, O God, the path whereon I go,
Bless to me, O God, the people whom I meet,
Today, tonight and tomorrow.

Ancient Celtic Prayer[3]

Morning Prayer

PROTECT, O LORD, from thoughts without
 action
Guard, O Lord, from words without feelings
Defend, O Lord, from ideas without results
And surround me with your Presence.

David Adam

O LIVING GOD, in whose presence I begin my
own day's living, I thank you that you are in
charge of today, and that I am utterly known
and understood by you. You guide and lead
me in the way that I should go, because you
love me and my whole world.

So, my Father, I bring to you my life today.
I long to make it an offering to you, as a day
well lived. But I so often use my time

wastefully or self-indulgently. So today, Father, help me:

– to turn vague good intentions into concrete action;

– to follow up ideas with the toil that makes them work;

– to keep my tongue from time-wasting,
   from self-indulgent gossip,
   from careless and insensitive words,
   from self-display.

O loving Father, how little I can achieve myself! But let me draw hope and strength minute by minute from your presence surrounding me and your love overshadowing me. And so, putting behind me all sense of inadequacy, let me glory today in the wonder of your love for us, the wisdom of your work for us, and the power of your purpose for us. In the name of our Lord Jesus whom you gave for us, let me share this day with others as a day you have made for us, in which to rejoice in your life and love. And so keep us thankful.

Ruth Etchells (adapted)

TEACH ME, O GOD, so to use all the circumstances of my life today that they may bring forth in me the fruits of holiness rather than the fruits of sin.

Let me use disappointments as material for patience:

Let me use success as material for thankfulness:

Let me use suspense as material for perseverance:

Let me use danger as material for courage:

Let me use reproach as material for long-suffering:

Let me use praise as material for humility:

Let me use pleasure as material for temperance:

Let me use pains as material for endurance.

John Baillie

Evening Prayer

Phos Hilaron

Hail, gladdening Light, of his pure glory
   poured,
Who is the immortal Father, heavenly, blest,
Holiest of Holies, Jesus Christ our Lord!

Now that we are come to the sun's hour of
   rest,
The lights of evening round us shine,
We hymn the Father, Son, and Holy Spirit
   divine.

Worthy are you at all times to be sung
With undefiled tongue,
Son of our God, giver of life, alone:
Therefore in all the world your glories,
Lord, they own.

Celebrating Common Prayer

The Apologist's Evening Prayer

FROM ALL MY lame defeats and oh! much
   more
From all the victories that I seemed to
   score;
From cleverness shot forth on Thy behalf
At which, while angels weep, the audience
   laugh;
From all my proofs of Thy divinity,
Thou, who wouldst give no sign, deliver me.
Thoughts are but coins. Let me not trust,
   instead
Of Thee, their thin-worn image of Thy head.
From all my thoughts,
even from my thoughts of Thee,
O thou fair Silence, fall, and set me free.
Lord of the narrow gate and the needle's eye,
Take from me all my trumpery lest I die.

C. S. Lewis

God's Will not Ours

An Answered Prayer

I ASKED FOR strength – and God gave me difficulties to make me strong.

I asked for wisdom – and God gave me problems to learn to solve.

I asked for prosperity – and God gave me brain and brawn to work.

I asked for courage – and God gave me dangers to overcome.

I asked for love – and God gave me troubled people to help.

I asked for favours – and God gave me opportunities.

I received nothing I wanted: I received everything I needed.

My prayer has been answered.

Author Unknown

DEAREST LORD, teach me to be generous;
Teach me to serve thee as thou deservest;
To give and not to count the cost,
To fight and not to heed the wounds,
To toil and not to seek for rest,
To labour and not to seek reward,
Save that of knowing that I do thy will.

St Ignatius Loyola

Jesus, Master Carpenter of Nazareth,
who on the cross through wood and nails
worked our whole salvation,
wield well your tools in this your workshop
    that I,
who come to you rough-hewn,
may by your hand be fashioned to a truer
    beauty
and a greater usefulness,
for the honour of your name.

Hal Pink

A Hymn to the Blessed
Virgin Mary

What shall we sing for Mary
The Mother of us all?
What shall we sing for the Virgin
Who heard the Angel's Call?
Sing Blessed is she who humbly
    obeyed
In whom God's will was done
Blessed the gift of joy she shared
In Jesus Christ her Son.

What shall we sing for Mary
The Mother of our Lord?
What shall we sing for the Virgin

Whose heart received the sword?
Sing Blessed is she who bravely obeyed
In whom God's will was done
Blessed the way of sorrow she shared
For Jesus Christ her Son.

What shall we sing for Mary
The Mother of our King?
What shall we sing for the Virgin
Which choirs of angels sing?
Sing Blessed is she who gladly obeyed
In whom God's will was done
Blessed the life of glory she shared
With Jesus Christ her Son.

Robert Willis

Trust in God

Psalm 23

THE LORD is my shepherd: therefore can I lack nothing.
He shall feed me in a green pasture: and lead me forth beside the waters of comfort.
   He shall convert my soul: and bring me forth in the paths of righteousness, for his Name's sake.

Yea, though I walk through the valley of the shadow of death, I will fear no evil: for thou art with me; thy rod and thy staff comfort me.

Thou shalt prepare a table before me against them that trouble me: thou hast anointed my head with oil, and my cup shall be full.

But thy loving-kindness and mercy shall follow me all the days of my life: and I will dwell in the house of the Lord for ever.

The Book of Common Prayer

AS CHILDREN bring their broken toys with tears
　　for us to mend.
I brought my broken dreams to God because
　　he was my friend.
But then instead of leaving him in peace to
　　work alone,
I hung around and tried to help with ways that
　　were my own.
At last I snatched them back and cried, 'How
　　can you be so slow?' –
'My child,' he said, 'What could I do? You
　　never did let go.'

Source Unknown

A WOMAN once dreamt she was in a big and very lovely church. There were no people in it, except herself, but the seats were piled high with parcels. They were all shapes and sizes, all carefully wrapped in different coloured wrappings, as if there was going to be a Christmas gift service! The woman was very puzzled. In her dream, an angel came to her, and she at once asked, 'Please tell me, what are all these parcels? Who are they for?' 'Ah,' said the angel, 'these are waiting to be collected. Some have been lying here a long time. They are the answers God is offering to people's prayers, but the people don't recognise them, or they don't like the shape or the wrappings, and so the parcels lie here, and the people go away saying that God hasn't answered their prayers.'

A Closer Walk With God

O JESUS
Be the canoe that holds me in the sea of life.
Be the steer that keeps me straight.
Be the outrigger that supports me in times of
    great temptation.
Let thy spirit be my sail that carries me
    through each day.

Keep my body strong,
so that I can paddle steadfastly on,
in the long voyage of life.

A New Hebridean Prayer

DEAR GOD, be good to me;
The sea is so wide,
And my boat is so small.

Breton Fisherman's Prayer

Lighting a Candle

Jesus said: 'I am the Light of the World.'

St John 9 v 5, RSV

He said: '... he who does what is true comes to the light, that it may be clearly seen that his deeds have been wrought in God'.

St John 3 v 21, RSV

He said: 'Then the kingdom of heaven shall be compared to ten maidens who took their lamps and went to meet the bridegroom. Five of them were foolish, and five were wise. For when the foolish took their lamps, they took no oil with them; but the wise took flasks of oil with their lamps'.

St Matthew 25 v 1–4, RSV

- a sign of Christ, the Light of the World;
- a sign of prayer for someone, and the offering of our lives;
- a reminder to others who may come here after us of our nearness to each other in prayer.

Christians throughout history have used candles to symbolise God's presence with us, and to enlighten worship. In recent years we have seen the growth in importance of light, as a sign of prayer, of freedom and of remembrance. Finding words to pray is sometimes difficult, often our hearts and minds are too heavy for mere words. Light a candle and allow the Holy Spirit to lead you in prayer. Pray with thanksgiving for those you know and remember, those in need, and the needs of the Church and the World.

A prayer card in the Lady Chapel of the
Abbey Church of St Mary the Virgin,
Sherborne

Peace

DEEP PEACE of the running wave to you.
Deep peace of the flowing air to you.
Deep peace of the quiet earth to you.
Deep peace of the shining stars to you.
Deep peace of the Son of Peace to you.

Celtic Benediction

PEACE, LORD, peace.
Help me by your peace
to give peace,
to radiate peace,
to receive peace,
to achieve peace.
Teach me by your peace
when to forego peace,
when to disturb peace,
when to distil peace,
always to be at peace,
O Lord of peace.

David Adam

85

Harvest

TAKE NO thought of the harvest
But only of proper sowing.

T.S. Eliot

ALL SEED-SOWING is a mysterious thing, whether the seed fall into the earth or into souls. Man is a husbandman; his whole work rightly understood is to develop life, to sow it everywhere. Such is the mission of humanity, and of this divine mission the great instrument is speech. We too often forget that language is both a seed-sowing and a revelation.

Henri Frederic Amiel

The Collect

ALMIGHTY and everlasting God,
we offer you our hearty thanks
for your fatherly goodness and care
in giving us the fruits of the earth in their
  seasons.
Give us grace to use them rightly,
  to your glory,

for our own well-being,
   and for the relief of those in need;
through Jesus Christ our Lord.

The Alternative Service Book

'WE DARE NOT ask you bless our harvest feast
Till it is spread for poorest and for least.
We dare not bring our harvest gifts to you
Unless our hungry brothers share them too.

Not only at this time, Lord; every day
Those whom you love are dying while we
   pray.
Teach us to do with less, and so to share
From our abundance more than we can spare.

Now with this harvest plenty round us piled,
Show us the Christ in every starving child;
Speak, as you spoke of old in Galilee,
You feed, or you refuse, not them but me!'

Lilian Cox

Rejecting Sin

God in Heaven, you have helped my life to
grow like a tree. Now something has hap-
pened. Satan, like a bird, has carried in one
twig of his own choosing after another.

Before I knew it he had built a dwelling-place and was living in it. Tonight, my Father, I am throwing out both the bird and the nest.

Prayer of a Nigerian Christian

A Petition for the 90s

WE THANK YOU for your love
We thank you for our life
We thank you for carers   But Lord!
A greater understanding and a better application for our needs would do us nicely.

You know of alienation, access, audibility and artificial joints
You know of braille and braillists and by-passes
You know of CCTVs* (NSMs* tend to get excluded)
     cornea and cochlea implants,
     counselling, chemotherapy, canes
     dialysis, and diminished responsibility employment
     finger spellers, flare paths* and fire regulations
     gadgets, glasses and grommet operations

We thank you for your love
We thank you for our life
We thank you for carers   But Lord!
A greater understanding and a better appli-
cation for our needs would do us nicely.

You know of hearing aids, hand rails, hymn
singing and house sales
        induction loops, information technology
        and infants
        lip readers, lifts, large print, limbs and
        libraries
        Ministers of Health, mobility, marked
        steps and
        Nursing Home sagas
        organs, and optical character recogni-
        tion systems*
        prescription charges, Perkins braillers
        and pollution

We thank you for your love
We thank you for our life
We thank you for carers   But Lord!
A greater understanding and a better appli-
cation for our needs would do us nicely.

You know of readers and reading, ramps,
relationships and research
        speech therapists, sign language and
        signers, self-threading needles, scanners,

sticks, specialist lighting and surgery

We thank you for your love
We thank you for our life
We thank you for carers   But Lord!
A greater understanding and a better application for our needs would do us nicely.

You know of translators, transport, training, transcribers,
> transplants and talking computers
> wheel chairs
> X-rays and – zero-rated tax!

So, Lord, how is it they don't? Don't they think it may be them?

And, Lord, while we're about it …
It would do us very nicely indeed not to think about rationing (didn't it go in the 50s?), selection processes, cut-backs and closures.
LAUDATE DOMINE

R.C.C.

* **CCTV** – closed circuit television magnifies print up to 60 times
NSM – Non Stipendiary Minister

Flare paths / tactile surfaces – a surface with small raised domes recommended by the Department of Transport

Optical Character Recognition Systems – an attachment to computers which converts print into braille, large print, or activates voice synthesizers

Psalm 138

I GIVE THEE THANKS, O Lord, with my whole heart; before the gods I sing thy praise;
I bow down toward thy holy temple and give thanks to thy name for thy steadfast love and thy faithfulness;
for thou hast exalted above everything thy name and thy word.
On the day I called, thou didst answer me, my strength of soul thou didst increase.
All the kings of the earth shall praise thee, O Lord,
for they have heard the words of thy mouth;
and they shall sing of the ways of the Lord, for great is the glory of the Lord.
For though the Lord is high, he regards the lowly;
but the haughty he knows from afar.
Though I walk in the midst of trouble, thou dost preserve my life;

thou dost stretch out thy hand against the
wrath of my enemies,
and thy right hand delivers me.
The Lord will fulfil his purpose for me;
thy steadfast love, O Lord, endures for ever.
Do not forsake the work of thy hands.

The Book of Common Prayer

3

WORK

Work for All

IDLENESS is the enemy of the soul. So have specific periods for manual labour.

The Rule of St Benedict 48 v 1

FAITH has set us on a journey
    past the landmarks that we know,
        taking risks with no insurance
            but the Word that tells us 'go!'
Friend or job or home or lover
    we may need to leave behind,
        outworn truths and ways of thinking,
            baggage to the past consigned.

Some are swags of easy conscience
    who with others hitch a ride,
        some are tourist-package Christians,
            dollar-safe, with Book and guide.
There are others on this journey –
    those who long and pray and search,
        heave the stones to free the structures,
            love the Christ and leave the Church.

We are this unlikely people
    in the body knit as one,
        company of clowns and cripples –
            some are wise and some can run.

Prophets are our travel agents,
   gospel-makers lay this road:
      to the place of peace and promise
      faith will take us into God.

                Shirley Erena Murray

The Unknown

I SAID TO the man who stood at the gate of the year, 'Give me a light that I may tread safely into the unknown'. And he replied: 'Go out into the darkness and put your hand into the hand of God. That shall be to you a better light and safer than a known way!' So I went forth and finding the hand of God, trod gladly into the night. And he led me towards the hills and the breaking of day in the lone East.

              Minnie Louise Haskins

I PRAY, LORD, that everything I do
may be prompted by your inspiration,
so that every prayer and work of mine
may begin from you
and be brought by you to completion.

           Based on the Prologue of
           The Rule of St Benedict

WE BELIEVE that the Divine Presence is everywhere, and that in every place the eye of the Lord is watching.

Proverbs 15 v 3

HELP ME to remember, Lord God,
that every day is your gift
and ought to be used according to your will.

Samuel Johnson

JESUS' HANDS were kind hands,
Doing good to all;
Healing pain and sickness,
Blessing children small;
Washing tired feet
And saving those who fall;
Jesus' hands were kind hands,
Doing good to all.
Take my hands, Lord Jesus,
Let them work for you,
Make them strong and gentle,
Kind in all I do;
Let me watch you, Jesus,
Till I'm gentle too,
Till my hands are kind hands,
Quick to work for you.

Margaret Cropper

DEAR LORD, may my mind become as a blank page. Put the thoughts into my head, the words into my mouth and guide my pen, so that, in however infinitesimal a way, I may be used as an instrument for good.

Robert Dougall

I ASK NOT to see
I ask not to know
I ask simply to be used

Cardinal Newman

LORD, TEACH me the way that you would have
    me go;
Lord, teach me the way that you would have
    me grow;
Lord, teach me the things you would have me
    know.
Lord, teach me the way that you would have
    me pray;
Lord, teach me the things that you would have
    me say;
Lord, teach me to stay forever close to you
    this day.

Jean Smith

GOD GIVE me work till my life shall end
And life till my work is done.

Epitaph of Winifred Holtby

Do ALL the good you can
By all the means you can
In all the ways you can
At all the times you can
To all the people you can
As long as you can.

Based on
The Rule of John Wesley

I SHALL pass through this world but once.
Therefore any good that I can do, any kind
   act
that I can perform for any fellow-creature, let
   me do it now.
Let me not delay, or omit it, for I shall not
   pass this way again.

Attributed to Etienne Giennet

Obedience

LORD OF LIGHT – shine on us;
Lord of peace – dwell in us;
Lord of might – succour us;
Lord of love – enfold us;
Lord of wisdom – enlighten us;
Then, Lord, let us go out as your witnesses,
in obedience to your command; to share the
good news of your mighty love for us in the
gift of your Son, our Saviour, Jesus Christ.

The Church in Wales

THE THINGS, good Lord, that we pray for,
give us the grace to labour for.

St Thomas More

ETERNAL GOD and Father, you create us by
your power and redeem us by your love:
guide and strengthen us by your spirit that
we may give ourselves in love and service to
one another and to you; through Jesus
Christ our Lord.

Celebrating Common Prayer

Trust

GOD HAS created me to do Him some definite service; He has committed some work to me which He has not committed to another. I have my mission – I may never know it in this life, but I shall be told it in the next. I am a link in a chain, a bond of connection between persons. He has not created me for naught. I shall do good, I shall do his work. I shall be an angel of peace, a preacher of truth in my own place *while not intending it –* if I do but keep his commandments.

Therefore I will trust Him. Whatever, wherever I am, I can never be thrown away. If I am in sickness, my sickness may serve Him; in perplexity, my perplexity may serve Him; if I am in sorrow, my sorrow may serve Him. He does nothing in vain. He knows what he is about. He may take away my friends, He may throw me among strangers. He may make me feel desolate, make my spirits sink, hide my future from me – still He knows what he is about.

Cardinal Newman

In the Home

LORD JESUS CHRIST, who taught your apostles to bless each home they entered with the words, 'Peace be to this house': I ask your blessing on the home of these your servants. Let your peace rest upon us, O Lord; keep us abiding in your love; and be with us in our going out and in our coming in, from this time forth for evermore.

Frank Colquhoun (adapted)

Children Learn What They Live

IF A CHILD lives with criticism
He learns to condemn.
If a child lives with hostility
He learns to fight.
If a child lives with ridicule
He learns to be shy.
If a child lives with shame
He learns to feel guilty.
If a child lives with tolerance
He learns to be patient.
If a child lives with encouragement
He learns confidence.
If a child lives with praise
He learns to appreciate.

If a child lives with fairness
He learns justice.
If a child lives with security
He learns to have faith.
If a child lives with approval
He learns to like himself.
If a child lives with acceptance
and friendship
He learns to find love in the world.

Church Book Room Press

Martha's Prayer

LORD, DEFEND me from feeling hard-done by
when the chores seem endless.
Forgive me when I am bored by the
    constantly recurring need to think about
    food.
Teach me to organize myself in order not
    to be rushed
but never to be ruled by organization
and always to have time to listen.
Make me laugh, not swear,
when the milk boils over.
Preserve me from getting in a fuss
when the Grand-Joneses are coming to
    dinner.
Let me thank you daily for my home, for
    warmth and food,

and for my friends and family.
Lord, remind me often that
it takes Martha as well as Mary
to serve you perfectly.

Clemency Greatorex

The Present Moment

LORD, I THANK you for teaching me how to live in the present moment. In this way I enjoy each simple task as I do it without thinking that I must hurry on to the next thing. I do what I am doing with all my ability and all my concentration. My mind is no longer divided, and life is more peaceful. Thank you for teaching me how to do this, and please help me how to show others the way to learn to trust you more completely and to do everything which has to be done at your time and your speed.

Michael Hollings and Etta Gullick

Avoid Hurrying

IN THE NAME of Jesus Christ, who was never in a hurry, we pray, O God, that thou wilt slow us down, for we know that we live too fast. With all eternity before us, make us take time to live – time to get acquainted with thee, time to enjoy thy blessings, and time to know each other.

Peter Marshall

TAKE TIME to read,
take time to think:
it is the road to wisdom.
Take time to laugh,
take time to love,
it is the road to being alive.
Take time to give,
take time to pray:
it is the way to God.

Christ was never in a hurry. And if God has given us anything to do for him, he will give time enough to finish it with a repose like Christ's.

Henry Drummond

IN OUR DAY TO DAY activities we are often busy doing things without stopping to reflect on the meaning of the Word of God for us. We often avoid the risk of listening to God's call by plunging into excessive activity. Hearing and doing are complementary in the role each one of us has to play. God has brought us into being both for our spiritual growth and to learn from one another.

Lord, we thank you for continuing to knock at our door. Help us to open at your call. Help us to listen to the words you now wish to speak in our hearts ... (pause) We have been restless, trying to accomplish our self-imposed tasks, setting aside your word, and going our own way. Lord, give us the courage to act. But let all that we do derive from your living Word.

Pray for us all, and especially for those called to serve as leaders in the Church that we may all give high priority to action that enables deeper and fuller communion between all Christians.

From *Prayer for Christian Unity, Day Five*, 1996

Workaholism

LORD TEMPER with tranquillity
Our manifold activity
That we may do our work for Thee
With very great simplicity.

A sixteenth-century prayer

'WORKAHOLISM' is a severe addiction. When we are busy, we feel we are needed. What happens to us when we can no longer be busy? People fall apart when they are made redundant, when they fall ill, when they can't find a job.

A Closer Walk With God

Administration!

Hymn and Prayer for Civil Servants

O THOU who seest all things below,
Grant that Thy servants may go slow,
That they may study to comply
With regulations till they die.

Teach us O Lord to reverence
Committees more than common sense;
To train our minds to make no plan
And pass the baby when we can.

So when the tempter seeks to give
Us feelings of initiative,
Or when alone we go too far,
Chastise us with a circular.

Mid war and tumult, fire and storms,
Give strength O Lord, to deal out forms.
Thus may Thy servants ever be
A flock of perfect sheep for Thee.

O, LORD, grant that this day we come to no
decisions, neither run we into any kind of
responsibility, but that all our doings may be
ordered to establish new departments, for
ever and ever.

Anon

Unemployment

OUR FATHER, in praying for the unemployed
we think especially of those who through no
fault of their own have lost their jobs and are

now searching for other work for the sake of their families.

May they not grow despondent or come to regard themselves as useless.

Help them to employ their skills and gifts in other directions and to find a measure of fulfilment in the service of the church or community till employment comes their way again.

Frank Colquhoun

Rest and Recreation

THE LORD is my pace-setter, I shall not
    rush,
He makes me stop and rest for quiet
    intervals,
he provides me with images of stillness,
    which restore my serenity.
He leads me in the way of efficiency;
    through calmness of mind.
And his guidance is peace.
Even though I have a great many things to
    accomplish each day
I will not fret, for his presence is here.
His timelessness, his all-importance will
    keep me in balance.

He prepares refreshment and renewal in
    the midst of activity.
By anointing my mind with his oils of
    tranquillity,
My cup of joyous energy overflows.
Surely harmony and effectiveness shall
    be the fruits of my hours
For I shall walk in the pace of my Lord,
    and dwell in his house for ever.

Toki Miyashina

In the Evening

ABIDE WITH US, O Lord, for it is toward
evening and the day is far spent; abide with
us, and with thy whole Church. Abide with us
in the evening of the day, in the evening of
life, in the evening of the world. Abide with
us and with all thy faithful ones, O Lord, in
time and eternity.

Lutheran Manual of Prayer

MAY HE support us all the day long, till the
shades lengthen, and the evening comes,
and the busy world is hushed, and the fever
of life is over, and our work is done! Then in

His mercy may He give us a safe lodging, and a holy rest, and peace at the last.

John Henry Newman

Night Work

GOD of the daylight and God of the dark, we commend to your loving care all those individuals who work at night – whether from necessity or choice – to maintain lines of communication and energy, to provide care and protection. We hold before you in prayer team workers and those in solitary occupations. May they know your presence and peace.

R.C.C.

4

THE LISTENING HEART

A Prayerful Routine

HAVE SPECIFIC times for prayerful reading.

The Rule of St Benedict 48 v 1

CHOOSE A suitable time for recollection and frequently consider the loving-kindness of God. Do not read to satisfy curiosity or to pass the time, but study such things as move your heart to devotion.

Thomas à Kempis

GUARD WHAT has been entrusted to you.

1 Timothy 6 v 20, RSV

EXAMINE YOURSELVES to see whether you are holding to your faith.

2 Corinthians 3 v 5, RSV

Bible Reading

ALL SCRIPTURE is inspired by God and profitable for teaching, for reproof, for correction and for training in righteousness.

2 Timothy 3 v 16, RSV

115

God speaks to us in different ways, and is no respecter of persons. But curiosity often hinders us in the reading of the Scriptures, for we try to examine and dispute over matters that we should pass over and accept in simplicity. If you desire to profit, read with humility, simplicity, and faith, and have no concern to appear learned. Ask questions freely, and listen in silence to the words of the Saints; hear with patience the parables of the fathers, for they are not told without good cause.

Thomas à Kempis

Bible Sunday, 2nd Sunday in Advent
The Collect

BLESSED LORD,
who caused all holy Scriptures
    to be written for our learning:
    help us so to hear them,
to read, mark, learn, and inwardly digest
    them
that, through patience, and the comfort
    of your holy word,
we may embrace and for ever hold fast
    the hope of everlasting life,
which you have given us in our Saviour
    Jesus Christ.

The Alternative Service Book

O LORD Jesus Christ, who as a child didst learn and didst grow in wisdom; Grant us so to learn thy holy Word, that we may walk in thy ways and daily grow more like unto thee, who livest and reignest with the Father and the Holy Ghost, one God, world without end. Amen.

Church of Ireland,
Book of Common Prayer

WHENEVER you read the Gospel Christ Himself is speaking to you. And while you read, you are praying and talking with him.

St Tikhon of Zadonsk

God's Timing

... being attentive to the times of the day; when the birds began to sing, and the deer came out of the morning fog, and the sun came up. The reason why we don't take time is a feeling that we have to keep moving. This is a real sickness. We live in the fullness of time. Every moment is God's own good time, his kairos. The whole thing boils down to giving ourselves in prayer a chance to

realise that we have what we seek. We don't
rush after it. It was there all the time, and if we
give it time, it will make itself known to us.

Thomas Merton

O GRACIOUS and holy Father,
give us wisdom to perceive thee,
diligence to seek thee,
patience to wait for thee,
eyes to behold thee,
a heart to meditate on thee,
and a life to proclaim thee;
through the power of the Spirit of Jesus
    Christ our Lord.

Frank Colquhoun

FAITH makes a Christian
Life proves a Christian
Trial confirms a Christian
Death crowns a Christian

Anon

Knowing Ourselves

I THANK YOU, Lord, for knowing me
better than I know myself,
and for letting me know myself

better than others know me.
Make me, I pray
better than they suppose,
and forgive me for what they do not know.

Source Unknown

Loving Myself

LOVING MYSELF means that I realise I am a person created by God.

I need to know myself as God knows me. So (I must) try to get to know myself as fully as possible. God knows who I am, loves and cares for me. So, I too need to know who I am, and to love and care for myself – because I am important to God.

A Closer Walk with God

Meditation

GOD BE IN my head and in my understanding.
God be in my eyes, and in my looking.
God be in my mouth, and in my speaking.
God be in my heart, and in my thinking.
God be at my end, and at my departing.

Book of Hours

IT IS NOT necessary that we should discover new ideas in our meditation. It is sufficient if the word as we read and understand it penetrates and dwells within us. As Mary pondered in her heart the tidings that were told by the shepherds, as what we have casually heard follows us for a long time, sticks in our mind, occupies, disturbs or delights us, without our ability to do anything about it, so in meditation God's word seeks to enter in and remain with us. It strives to stir us to work and to operate in us so that we shall not get away from it the whole day long. Then it will do its work in us without our being aware of it.

Dietrich Bonhoeffer

LORD,
I pray for all those whose lives have
    touched mine,
for good or evil,
in the past or in the present,
whether they are alive or departed.
give them an abundance of your grace in
    this world,
and in eternity may they find joy in your
    presence,
in the name of Jesus the Lord.

Alan Rees OSB

I AM ONLY a spark:
make me a fire.
I am only a string:
make me a lyre.
I am only a drop:
make me a fountain.
I am only an anthill:
make me a mountain.
I am only a feather:
make me a wing.
I am only a rag:
make me a king!

A Mexican Prayer

MIRACLES may show me the saint, they do not show me how he became a saint: and that is what I want to see. It is not the completed process that intrigues me: it is the process itself: for you see, my work is not to be a saint. Tell me what was churning in his soul as he battled his way up from selfishness and the allurements of sin to the great heart of God.

M Raymond, OCSO

MEN GO abroad to wonder at the height of mountains, at the huge waves of the sea, at the long courses of the rivers, at the vast compasses of the ocean, at the circular motion of the stars, and they pass by themselves without wondering.

St Augustine

Here is a Man

HERE IS a man who was born in an obscure village, the child of a peasant woman. He worked in a carpenter's shop until he was thirty, and then for three years he was an itinerant preacher. He had no credentials but himself. While still a young man, the tide of popular opinion turned against him. His friends – the twelve men who had learned so much from him, and had promised him their enduring loyalty – ran away, and left him. He went through a mockery of a trial; he was nailed upon a cross between two thieves; when he was dead, he was taken down and laid in a borrowed grave through the pity of a friend.

Yet I am well within the mark when I say that all the armies that ever marched, and all the parliaments that ever sat, and all the kings that ever reigned, put together, have not affected the life of man upon this earth as has this one solitary life.

Anon seventeenth century

THERE ARE many worlds and many states, but God is a transworld reality. God is the God of every world, and the Lord of every state. God is many and yet one, and in God there are many worlds yet one. God does not abolish darkness; God is the Lord of both light and darkness. If in God's light we see light, then in God's darkness we see darkness. If a journey into light is a journey into God, then a journey into darkness is a journey into God. This is why I go on journeying, not through, but into.

John M. Hull [5]

Ash Wednesday

From Lent to New Life

He was in the wilderness 40 days
(St Mark 1 v 13).

TODAY, Ash Wednesday, marks the beginning of Lent, the 40 days of spiritual discipline that lead up to Easter. In the 18th century Dean Swift, the author of *Gulliver's Travels*, wrote that he hated Lent. 'I hate different diets and furmity and butter, and herb porridge; and sour devout faces of people who only put on religion for seven weeks.' Swift's response was in contrast to that of George Herbert, one of whose poems about the Lenten fast begins 'Welcome! *Feast* of Lent'.

The 40 days marked the time of Jesus's own testing in the wilderness, graphically described as a wrestling, a conflict, with Satan, the tempter, a conflict concerned as much with motive as with method – turning stones into bread; casting himself down from the pinnacle of the Temple; not being deflected into the worship of the tempter; gaining the whole world and losing his own soul. In the Christian Year the 40 days lead up to Holy Week and Easter, to the great conflict of good and evil, light and darkness, where death and life contend in the passion and death of Christ. The English called this season Lent, a word which means 'spring', the time when the days are lengthening, a time of resurrection and new life springing from the darkness of death.

The sign of Ash Wednesday is the smudge of ash on the forehead, a reminder that we are dust and to dust we shall return. The end of our human journey is the dust of death, for many today literally the scattering of ashes. And ashes for the Old Testament were the sign of repentance. The sinner sat in sackcloth and ashes, an ascetic, penitential discipline.

Asceticism is no longer a popular word. It has a negative connotation, as if it were simply a distortion of the human spirit. Yet *ascesis*, the Greek word from which it derives, means simply 'training' or 'exercise', and we applaud and encourage the need for training, in sport, in music, and in business. The ascetic discipline of the spiritual life is neglected at our peril. We need to remember our mortality. We need to stand back and take stock. We need to cleanse our perceptions; to ask questions about the good, what it is and how we serve it, about the values that our lives express. Lent challenges our greed and our grasping. It is a time for looking hard at our attachments and addictions, and a time for finding space that we may attend to the searching love of God.

Jesus spent 40 days in the wilderness. Later on Christian monks went to the Egyptian desert, which they called 'the place of the weighing of the heart', to find a freedom from the choking cares of the world's frenetic activity, and a space to discover the peace of God that passes all understanding.

125

Our need today is no less great. We delude ourselves if we consider only the education we all need at every age to be simply a matter of acquiring techniques and information; it is also, and most importantly, about learning wisdom, and that spiritual wisdom demands both penitence and humility. Without it we may gain the whole world and lose our own souls. Ash Wednesday's reminder that we are dust is to lead us into the springtime of Lent and the new life of Easter.

A Leader – *The Times*,
21 February 1996

Listening

TEACH US to listen, Lord
to one another with enjoyment and
   especially:
to the diffident, with encouragement;
to the repetitive, with patience;
to the sad, with understanding;
to the happy, joyfully;
to the aggressive, calmly;
and to the gossip – never.

And above all, Lord
teach us to listen to you with our hearts.

Clemency Greatorex

LORD, SHOW us deeply how important it is to
be useless.

Bangkok Prayer

WINTER IS neither death
nor even slumber.
Winter is the season of our growth.

Donald Hilton

LIFE CAN only be understood backwards; but
it must be lived forwards.

Soren Kierkegaard

MEDITATION is not having great thoughts, but
loving the words you hear and letting them
shape you.

A Closer Walk With God

INSTEAD of taking the words apart, we
should bring them together in our innermost
being; instead of wondering if we agree or
disagree, we should wonder which words

are directly spoken to us and connect directly with our most personal story. Instead of thinking about the words as an interesting subject for a sermon or discussion, we must be willing to let them penetrate into the most hidden corners of our heart, even to those places where no other word has yet found entrance. Then and then only can the word bear fruit as seed sown in rich soil. Only then can we really hear and understand.

Henri Nouwen

Acceptance

The Serenity Prayer

O GOD give me serenity to accept what
   cannot be changed;
courage to change the things I can;
and the wisdom to know the difference.

Reinhold Niebuhr

Victims of War

I DON'T WANT to have lived in vain like most people. I want to be useful, or bring enjoyment to people, even those I have never met. I want to go on living even after my death and that's why I'm grateful to God for having given me this gift which I can use to develop and to express all that's inside me.

Anne Frank[6]

Today

FROM TOMORROW on I shall be sad,
from tomorrow on.
Not today. Today I will be glad.

And every day,
no matter how bitter it may be,
I shall say;
From tomorrow on I shall be sad,
not today.

An Anonymous Child
in a Nazi Death Camp

Victims of Society

MS KWON stands before the dead bodies of her three daughters. The girls have left the family with a hope for happiness for Jaeman, their brother. No more will they cause concern to the poor struggling family.

Ms Kwon's story is common in many Asian communities, both rural and urban. She has given birth to girls, a pity for everyone in the family. In order to have 'a boy please' she has ended up with four daughters.

The girls gradually discovered they were considered a bad omen and the root cause of the problems the family was encountering. It took them little time to decide that the solution to all problems was to end their own lives.

Ms Kwon's daughters are the victims of a society where women cannot maintain their human dignity and worth.

Harold Williams

Comfort

A Good Night's Sleep

SLEEP IS something we take for granted until we don't have it. Then, rather like happiness, the more we consciously seek it, the more it escapes us. Only those who lack it seem properly to appreciate it, like Macbeth:

Innocent sleep,
Sleep that knits up the ravell'd sleeve of
  care,
The death of each day's life, sore labour's
  bath
Balm of hurt minds, great nature's second
  course
Chief nourisher in life's feast.

There is an obvious analogy between going to sleep and dying, as there is between waking up and resurrection. This no doubt accounts for the New Testament view that the Christian dead, awaiting the imminent Last Things, are sleeping in Christ ... Just as it would be intolerable if this life went on and on for ever, so it would be equally intolerable if day were not bounded by night, and consciousness by sleep. On this view, sleep is a kind of mini-death, and

every awakening a mini-resurrection. Night
and morning we anticipate our future des-
tiny. I find this a fruitful subject for meditation, especially in Easter week.

Hugh Montefiore

THE DAY is done, and the darkness
Falls from the wings of Night,
As a feather is wafted downward
From an eagle in his flight.

Henry Wadsworth Longfellow

AND IF TONIGHT my soul may find her
    peace
in sleep, and sink in good oblivion,
and in the morning wake like a new-
    opened flower
then I have been dipped again in God,
    and new created ...

And if, in the changing phases of man's
    life
I fall in sickness and in misery
my wrists seem broken and my heart
    seems dead
and strength is gone, and my life
is only the leavings of a life:

And still, among it all, snatches of lovely oblivion, and snatches of renewal, odd, wintry flowers upon the withered stem, yet new, strange flowers such as my life has not brought forth before, new blossoms of me –

then I must know that still
I am in the hands (of) the unknown God,
he is breaking me down to his own oblivion
to send me forth on a new morning, a new
 man.

D. H. Lawrence[7]

Avoiding Sin

DO NOT BE anxious; do not fight your thoughts, or attempt to answer any doubts that the Devil suggests: trust in God's word, believe His saints and prophets, and the wicked enemy will flee from you. Often it is very profitable that the servant of God should experience such doubts, since the Devil does not tempt unbelievers and sinners who are already his own; but he tempts and vexes the faithful and devout in every way he can.

Thomas à Kempis

The Blind

Earthly Sight and Heavenly Sight[8]

LORD CHRIST, when you gave sight to the blind in your ministry on earth you spoke about a greater power of inward sight: we pray that those who cannot see the world about them may perceive the things of eternal worth, and receive from those near to them a friendship and care which will help them to overcome their handicap and will be a light to their path.

New Every Morning

God's Activity in Us

YET, O LORD, you are our Father.
We are the clay, and you are the potter;
we are all the work of your hand.

Isaiah 64 v 8, NIV

GO DOWN to the potter's house, and there I will give you my message. So I went down to the potter's house, and I saw him working at the wheel. But the pot he was shaping from the clay was marred in his hands; so the potter formed it into another pot, shaping it as seemed best to him.

Jeremiah 18 v 2–4, NIV

What the Donkey Saw

NO ROOM in the inn, of course,
And not that much in the stable,
What with the shepherds, Magi, Mary,
Joseph, the heavenly host –
Not to mention the baby
Using our manger as a cot.
You couldn't have squeezed another
    cherub in
For love or money.

Still, in spite of the overcrowding,
I did my best to make them feel wanted.
I could see the baby and I
Would be going places together.

U. A. Fanthorpe

What is God?

Footprints

ONE NIGHT I dreamed a dream.
I was walking along the beach with my Lord.
Across the dark sky flashed scenes from my life.
For each scene, I noticed two sets of
footprints in the sand,
One belonging to me and one to my Lord.
When the last scene of my life shot before me
I looked back at the footprints in the sand
and to my surprise,
I noticed that many times along the path of my
life
there was only one set of footprints.
I realised that this was at the lowest and
saddest times of my life.
This always bothered me
and I questioned the Lord about my dilemma.
'Lord, you told me when I decided to follow You,
You would walk and talk with me all the way.
But I'm aware that during the most
troublesome
Times of my life there is only one set of
footprints.
I just don't understand why, when I needed
you most,
You leave me.'

He whispered, 'My precious child,
I love you and will never leave you,
Never, ever, during your trials and testings.
When you saw only one set of footprints,
It was then that I carried you.'

Margaret Fishback Powers

A LONELY walk,
A quiet talk,
A grain of sand,
A soft white hand,
A child's new toy,
A moment's joy,
A new day's dawn,
A tottering fawn,
A cloud above,
Spring's young love,
A breath of air,
A silent prayer,
A gentle nod,
This is God.

Robert M. Warner

5

HOSPITALITY

Sincerity

NEVER GIVE a hollow greeting of peace
or turn away when someone needs your love

The Rule of St Benedict
4 vv 25–6

DO NOT FORGET to entertain strangers, for by doing so some people have entertained angels without knowing it.

Hebrews 13 v 2, NIV

JESUS SAID: 'And whoever gives to one of these little ones even a cup of cold water because he is a disciple, truly, I say to you, he shall not lose his reward.'

Matthew 10 v 42, RSV

One Family in Christ

CHURCH is just a building
with steeples
CH   CH
unless UR there

Ray Divall

ACROSS the barriers that divide race from
   race:
Reconcile us, O Christ, by your cross.
Across the barriers that divide the rich from
   the poor:
Reconcile us, O Christ, by your cross.
Across the barriers that divide people of
   different faiths:
Reconcile us, O Christ, by your cross.
Across the barriers that divide Christians:
Reconcile us, O Christ, by your cross.
Across the barriers that divide men and
   women, young and old:
Reconcile us, O Christ, by your cross.
Confront us, O Christ, with the hidden pre-
judices and fears which deny and betray our
prayers. Enable us to see the causes of
strife. Remove from us all false sense of
superiority. Teach us to grow in unity with all
God's children.

The World Council of Churches

IS IT NOT to share your food with the hungry
and to provide the poor wanderer with
   shelter . . .

Isaiah 58 v 7, NIV

O GOD, make the door of this house wide enough, to receive all who need human love and fellowship; narrow enough to shut out all envy, pride, and strife. Make its threshold smooth enough to be no stumbling block to children, or to straying feet, but rugged and strong to turn back the tempter's power. God, make the doorway of this house the entrance to your eternal kingdom.

Thomas Ken

Smile

A SMILE COSTS nothing but bestows much. It enriches those who receive without impoverishing those who give. It takes only a moment, yet the memory of it can last for ever. It spreads happiness in the home and promotes goodwill at work. Yet it cannot be bought, begged, or stolen, for it is of no value to anyone until it is given away. Some people are too world-weary to smile. Give them one of yours, for no one needs a smile as much as those who have none to give.

Source Unknown

I SAW A stranger today
I put food for him in the eating-place
And drink in the drinking-place
And music in the listening-place.
In the Holy Name of the Trinity
He blessed myself and my house
My goods and my family.
And the lark said in her warble
Often, often, often
Goes Christ in the Stranger's guise
O, oft and oft and oft,
Goes Christ in the Stranger's guise.

A rune of hospitality

Graces

COME LORD Jesus be our guest,
And may our meal by thee be blest.

Martin Luther

BLESS, O LORD, this food to our use and
ourselves to thy service, and make us mind-
ful of the needs of others, for Christ's sake.

Anon

LORD, TODAY you made us known to friends
  we did not know,
And you have given us seats in homes
  which are not our own.
You have brought the distant near,
And made a brother of a stranger,
Forgive us Lord . . .
We did not introduce you.

Prayer from Polynesia

EVEN AS the water falls on the dry tea leaves
and brings out their flavour, so may your
spirit fall on us too, so that we may bring
refreshment and joy to others.

Source Unknown

Agapé[9]

BE GENTLE, when you touch bread,
Let it not be uncared for, unwanted.
So often bread is taken for granted.
There is so much beauty in bread,
Beauty of sun and soil,
Beauty of patient toil.
Winds and rain have caressed it,
Christ often blessed it;
Be gentle when you touch bread.

Be loving when you drink wine,
So freely received and joyfully shared
In the spirit of Him who cared;
Warm as a flowing river,
Shining as clear as the sun,
Deep as the soil
Of human toil,
The winds and air caressed it,
Christ often blessed it,
Be loving when you drink wine.

Source Unknown

O LORD,
our meal is steaming before us,
and it smells very good.
The water is clear and fresh.
We are happy and satisfied.
But now we must think of our sisters
and brothers all over the world
who have nothing to eat
and only a little to drink.
Please, please let them have enough
    to eat
and enough to drink.
This is most important;
but give them also
what they need every day
in order to get through this life.

Just as you gave enough to eat and drink
to the people of Israel in the desert,
please give it also
to our hungry and thirsty brothers and
  sisters,
now and at any time.

An African Christian

ˉime for Children, and what they can teach us

CONTACT WITH children teaches us sincerity, simplicity, the habit of living in the present hour, the present action. Children are, as it were, reborn daily: hence their spontaneity, the lack of complexity in their souls, the simplicity of their judgements and actions.

Moreover, their intuitive distinctions between good and evil are unencumbered, their souls are free of the bonds of sin, they are not under the necessity of weighing and analysing. We possess all this as a birthright which we wantonly scatter on our way, so that we must afterwards painfully gather up the fragments of our lost fortune.

Father Alexander Elchaninov

BETWEEN THE dark and the daylight,
When the night is beginning to lower,
Comes a pause in the day's occupations,
That is known as the Children's Hour.

Henry Wadsworth Longfellow

AND NATURE, the old Nurse, took
The child upon her knee,
Saying 'Here is a story book
Thy father hath written for thee.

'Come wander with me,' she said,
'Into regions yet untrod,
And read what is still unread
In the Manuscripts of God.'

And he wandered away and away
With Nature, the dear old Nurse,
Who sang to him night and day
The rhymes of the universe.

Henry Wadsworth Longfellow

Being a Neighbour

ANYONE WHO has entered into the darkness of
another's pain, loss or bewilderment, and without the benefit of detached professionalism,

will know the feeling of wanting to escape, of wishing they had not become involved. Caring is costly, unsettling, even distasteful at times. The valley of deep shadows in another person's life frightens us too, and we need courage and constancy to enter it.

Kenneth Leach

Pilgrims in Mexico

'WHO KNOCKS at my door, so late in the night?'

'We are pilgrims, without shelter, and we want only a place to rest.'

'Go somewhere else and disturb me not again.'

'But the night is very cold. We have come from afar, and we are very tired.'

'But who are you? I know you not.'

'I am Joseph of Nazareth, a carpenter, and with me is Mary, my wife, who will be the mother of the Son of God.'

'Then come into my humble home, and welcome! And may the Lord give shelter to my soul when I leave this world!'

Traditional

1 WHEN I NEEDED a neigbour, were you there,
    were you there?
When I needed a neighbour, were you
    there?

Chorus
And the creed and the colour and the name
    won't matter,
were you there?

2 I was hungry and thirsty, were you there,
    were you there?
I was hungry and thirsty, were you there?

3 I was cold, I was naked, were you there,
    were you there?
I was hungry and thirsty, were you there?

4 When I needed a shelter, were you there,
    were you there?
When I needed a shelter,
    were you there?

5 When I needed a healer, were you there,
    were you there?
When I needed a healer, were you there?

6 Wherever you travel, I'll be there,
    I'll be there,
wherever you travel, I'll be there,

And the creed and the colour and the name
  won't matter,
I'll be there.

Sydney Carter

The Environment

THE FOREST is our livelihood. We have lived here before any of you outsiders came. We fished in clean rivers and hunted in the jungle. We made our sago meat and ate fruit of trees. Our life was not easy but we lived in content. Now the logging companies turn rivers into muddy streams and the jungle into devastation. The fish cannot survive in dirty rivers and wild animals will not live in devastated forests. You took advantage of our trusting nature and cheated us into unfair deals. By your doing, you have taken away our livelihood and threaten our very lives. We want our ancestral land, the land we live on, back. We can use it in a wiser way. When you come to us, come as guests, with respect.

Declaration of The Penan People
Borneo

The Stricken Elm

OH LOVELY tree no more will be seen
Your spreading branches clothed in green,
  No more will children play in your shade
    again,
Or old men shelter from the rain.
No more from thee the blackbirds song
Sounding out at early dawn.
You have stood for many years in storm and
  sun
But now old friend your day is done
So farewell old majestic tree
And grateful thanks to the one who planted
  thee.

                              Ted Ashley

  GOD BLESS the field and bless the furrow
  Stream and branch and rabbit burrow
  Hill and stone and flower and tree
  From Bristol Town to Weatherby
  Bless the sun and bless the street
  Bless the night and bless the day
  From Somerset and all the way
  To the meadows of Cathay.

  Bless the minnow, bless the whale
  Bless the rainbow and the hail
  Bless the nest and bless the leaf

Bless the righteous and the thief
Bless the wind and bless the fin
Bless the air I travel in
Bless the mill and bless the mouse
Bless the miller's bricken house
Bless the earth and bless the sea
God bless you and God bless me.

Traditional

Animals

THE BLISS of the animals lies in this, that, on
their lower level, they shadow the bliss of
those – few at any moment on the earth –
who do not 'look before and after, and pine
for what is not' but live in the holy careless-
ness of the eternal now.

George Macdonald

The Ass

I WOKE and rose and slipt away
To the heathery hills in the morning grey.

In a field where the dew lay cold and deep
I met an ass, new roused from sleep.

I stroked his nose and I tickled his ears,
And spoke soft words to quiet his fears.

His eyes stared into the eyes of me
And he kissed my hands of his courtesy.

'O big, brown brother out of the waste,
How do thistles for breakfast taste?

'And do you rejoice in the dawn divine
With a heart that is glad no less than mine?

'For, brother, the depth of your gentle eyes
Is strange and mystic as the skies:

'What are the thoughts that grope behind,
Down in the mist of a donkey mind?

'Can it be true, as the wise men tell,
That you are a mask of God as well,

'And, as in us, so in you no less
Speaks the eternal Loveliness.

'And words of the lips that all things know
Among the thoughts of a donkey go?

'However it be, O four-foot brother,
Fair today is the earth, our mother.

'God send you peace and delight thereof,
And all green meat of the waste you love,

'And guard you well from violent men
Who'd put you back in the shafts again.'

But the ass had far too wise a head
To answer one of the things I said,

So he twitched his fair ears up and down
And turned to nuzzle his shoulder brown.

C. S. Lewis

The Dog's Prayer

O LORD of all creatures, make the man, my master, as faithful to other men as I am to him. Make him as loving to his family and friends as I am to him. Make him the honest guardian to the blessings which you have entrusted to him as I honestly guard his own. Give him, O Lord, an easy and spontaneous smile, easy and spontaneous as when I wag my tail. May he be as readily grateful as I am quick to lick his hand. Grant him patience equal to mine, when I await his return without complaining. Give him my courage, my readiness to sacrifice everything for him in all circumstances, even life itself. Keep for him the youthfulness of my heart and the cheerfulness of my thoughts. O Lord of all

creatures, as I am always truly a dog, grant
that he may be always truly a man.

Pero Scanziani[10]

WHO'S THIS – alone with stone and sky?
It's only my old dog and I –
It's only him; it's only me;
Alone with stone and grass and tree.

What share we most – we two together?
Smells, and awareness of the weather.
What is it makes us more than dust?
My trust in him; in me his trust.

Here's anyhow one decent thing
That life to man and dog can bring;
One decent thing, remultiplied
Till earth's last dog and man have died.

Siegfried Sassoon

A Cat

WHY DID THEY turn me out?
I whispered – I didn't shout.
I *wanted* to be there
with a little feline prayer.
But although I didn't shout,
They turned me out.

I don't believe they knew,
That a hushed up mew
is the best a cat can do.
So – although it wasn't a shout,
They turned me out.

And the end of my prayer was said
Outside – on the mat – instead.

Sister Maud CAH

Wild birds

MY SACRAMENT of wine and broken bread
Is now prepared, and ready to be done;
The Tit shall hold a crust with both his feet,
While, crumb by crumb, he picks it like a
    bone.
The Thrush, ashamed of his thin ribs, has
    blown
His feathers out, to make himself look fat;
The Robin, with his back humped twice as
    high,
For pity's sake – has crossed my threshold
    mat.
The Sparrow's here, the Finch and Jenny
    Wren,
The wine is poured, the crumbs are white
    and small –

And when each little mouth has broken
   bread —
Shall I not drink and bless them one and all?

W. H. Davies

Trust

NOAH walked with God

Genesis 6 v 9, RSV

BY FAITH Noah, being warned by God concerning events as yet unseen, took heed and constructed an ark for the saving of his household; by this he condemned the world and became an heir of the righteousness which comes by faith.

Hebrews 11 v 7, RSV

AND GOD SAID, 'This is the sign of the covenant I am making between me and you and every living creature with you, a covenant for all generations to come: I set my rainbow in the clouds, and it will be the sign of the covenant between me and the earth. Whenever I bring clouds over the earth and the rainbow appears in the clouds, I will remember my covenant between me and you and all living creatures of every kind. Never again will the waters become a flood to destroy all life.'

Genesis 9 v 12–15, NIV

Focus on Christ

MY CROSS is a rainbow coloured cross,
Violet, Indigo, Blue, Green, Yellow, Orange,
    Red,
Colours of the rainbow,
A rainbow showed centuries ago to Noah
In a promise never to destroy life again
In a promise fulfilled two thousand years
    ago.
Redeeming humankind
On the cross.

My cross is a rainbow coloured cross
To liberate all,
North and South, East and West,
Black and White, Yellow and Brown.
Male and Female.

My cross is a rainbow coloured cross,
For I am blue with the pain of oppression

And blue with the struggle for freedom
And green with hope.

As I walk the royal (violet) road of liberation
With flowers yellow, orange and red,
Springing up in celebration,
Of new life
Creating a new Spring,
Of eternal liberation
In the Resurrection of Christ.

Judith Sequeira

AND THOSE who do not carry their cross and
follow me cannot be my disciples.

St Luke 14 v 27, NIV

I CARRY a cross in my pocket:
a simple reminder to me
of the fact that I am a Christian
no matter where I may be.
This little cross is not magic,
nor is it a good luck charm.
It isn't meant to protect me
from every physical harm.
It's not for identification
for all the world to see.
It's simply an understanding
between my Saviour and me.

It reminds me, too, to be thankful
for my blessings day by day,
and to strive to serve him better
in all that I do and say.
It's also a daily reminder
of the peace and comfort I share
with all who know my Master
and give themselves to his care.
So, I carry a cross in my pocket
reminding no one but me
that Jesus Christ is the Lord of my life,
if only I'll let him be.

Kevin Mayhew

A Blessing for Departing Guests

MAY THE ROAD rise with you
May the wind always be at your back
May the sun shine warm upon your face
And the rain fall soft upon your fields
And, until we meet again,
May God keep you in the hollow of his
    hand.

6

THE COMMUNITY SPIRIT

The Will of God

MY SON, let this be your constant prayer: 'Lord, if this be your will, so let it be. Lord, if this is good and profitable, give me grace to use it to your glory. But if it be hurtful and injurious to my soul's health, then remove this desire from my mind, I pray.'

Thomas à Kempis

LORD of creation to you be all praise!
Most mighty your working, most wondrous
   your ways!
Your glory and might are beyond us to tell,
and yet in the heart of the humble you dwell.

Lord of all power, I give you my will,
in joyful obedience your tasks to fulfil.
Your bondage is freedom, your service is
   song,
and, held in your keeping, my weakness is
   strong.

Lord of all wisdom, I give you my mind,
rich truth that surpasses man's knowledge to
   find.
What eye has not seen and what ear has
   not heard
is taught by your Spirit and shines from your
   Word.

Lord of all bounty, I give you my heart;
I praise and adore you for all you impart:
your love to inspire me, your counsel to
    guide,
your presence to cheer me, whatever betide.

Lord of all being, I give you my all;
if e'er I disown you I stumble and fall;
but, sworn in glad service your word to obey,
I walk in your freedom to the end of the way.

Jack C. Winslow

The Welfare of Others

DO NOT WITHHOLD good from those to whom
it is due, when it is in your power to do it.

Proverbs 3 v 27, RSV

City Life

BUT SEEK the welfare of the city where I have
sent you into exile, and pray to the Lord on
its behalf, for in its welfare you will find your
welfare.

Jeremiah 29 v 7, RSV

GOD OF THE CITY, God of the tenement and
the houses of the rich, God of the subway
and the night-club, God of the cathedral and

the streets, God of the sober and the drunk, the junkie and the stripper, the gambler and the good family man; dear God, help us to see the world and its children through your eyes, and to love accordingly.

Monica Furlong

Offenders

CHRIST OUR LORD, friend of outcasts and sinners, grant to all offenders against the law the gift of repentance and the knowledge of your forgiveness; and so renew a right spirit within them that they may find true joy and freedom in your service.

New Every Morning

O GOD GIVE ME the strength to look up and not down, to look forward and not back, to look out and not in and to lend a hand.

Short Prayers for the Long Day

LET US behave gently,
that we may die peacefully;
That our children may stretch out their
    hands
upon us in burial.

Yoruba

SO THEN, as we have opportunity let us do good to all men, and especially to those who are of the household of faith.

Galatians 6 v 10, RSV

Seed Silence

LORD, MAKE the old tolerant,
the young sympathetic, the great humble,
  the busy patient,
Make rich people understanding,
strong people gentle,
those who are weak prayerful;
make the religious lovable,
happy folk thoughtful, the clever kindly,
the bad good,
the good pleasant
and, dear Lord, make me what I ought to be.

Short Prayers for the Long Day

God Calling

THERE IS AN old Christian tradition that God sends each person into this world with a special message to deliver with a special song to sing for others with a special act of love to bestow.

J. Powell

CHRIST HAS no body now on earth but yours, no hands but yours, no feet but yours.

Yours are the eyes through which must look out Christ's compassion on the world.

Yours are the feet with which He is to go about doing good.

Yours are the hands with which He is to bless men now.

St Teresa of Avila

TWO MEN please God –
he who serves him with all his heart
because he knows him.
he who seeks him with all his heart
because he knows him not.

Lord, when I look at life
may I see through your eyes,
sensitively.

Lord, when I hear men speak
may I listen with your ears,
attentively.

Lord, when I speak to men
may I use your words,
thoughtfully.

Lord, when I use my hands
may I give your hands,
caringly.

Lord, as I live each day
may I walk with you,
lovingly.

Short Prayers for the Long Day

GUARD MY EYES, O Lord,
so that seeing other people's wealth
will not make me covetous.
Guard my ears,
so that they will not listen to foolish and
    malicious gossip.
Guard my heart,
so that I shall not take pleasure
in the temptations of the world.
Guard my hands,
so that they will not be used for violence
or for exploiting others.
Guard my feet upon the gentle earth,
so that in the bustle of life
I shall not forget the values of rest.

Based on a traditional
Irish prayer

O FATHER, give us the humility which
Realises its ignorance,
Admits its mistakes,
Recognises its need,
Welcomes advice,
Accepts rebuke.
Help us always
To praise rather than to criticise,
To sympathise rather than to condemn,
To encourage rather than to discourage,
To build rather than to destroy,
And to think of people at their best rather
    than at their worst.
This we ask for thy name's sake.

William Barclay

Stability

WHAT IS IT then to be stable? It seems to me that it may be described in the following terms: You will find stability at the moment when you discover that God is everywhere, that you do not need to seek Him elsewhere, that He is here, and if you do not find Him here it is useless to go and search for Him elsewhere because it is not Him that is absent from us, it is we who are absent from Him ... It is important to recognize that it is useless to seek God somewhere else. If you cannot find Him here you will not find Him anywhere else. This is important because it is only at the moment that you recognize this that you can truly find the fullness of the Kingdom of God in all its richness within you; that God is present in every situation and every place, that you will be able to say: 'So then I shall stay where I am.'

Metropolitan Anthony Bloom

High Office

ALMIGHTY GOD, we pray for those who hold unique positions of authority, trust and responsibility. May each person, both in their public and private roles, uphold the glory of your kingdom in our own nation and across the world. Help us to recognise the loneliness in courageous leadership, and we pray that all that they think, say, and do may be for the furtherance of your kingdom, here on earth.

R.C.C.

To BE HONEST, to be kind – to earn a little and to spend a little less, to make upon the whole a family happier for his presence, to renounce when that shall be necessary and not to be embittered, to keep a few friends ... above all ... to keep friends with himself – here is a task for all that a man has of fortitude and delicacy.

Robert Louis Stevenson

Peace

LORD, MAKE me an instrument of your peace.
Where there is hatred, let me sow love;
where there is injury, pardon;
where there is doubt, faith;
where there is despair, hope;
where there is darkness, light;
where there is sadness, joy;
O Divine Master, grant that I may not so much
seek to be consoled as to console,
to be understood as to understand,
to be loved as to love.
For it is in giving that we receive,
it is in pardoning that we are pardoned,
and it is in dying that we are born to eternal life.

Celebrating Common Prayer

Ideals

BLESSED IS HE who carries within himself a God, an ideal of beauty, and who obeys it; ideal of art, ideal of science, ideal of the fatherland, ideal of the virtues of the Gospel, for therein lie the springs of great thoughts and great actions; they all reflect light from the Infinite.

Louis Pasteur

Education

WE TEACH religion all day long.
We teach it in arithmetic, by accuracy.
We teach it in language, by learning to say what we mean – yea, yea or nay, nay.
We teach it in history, by humanity.
We teach it in geography, by breadth of mind.
We teach it in handicraft, by thoroughness.
We teach it in astronomy, by reverence.
We teach it by good manners to one another, and by truthfulness in all things.
We teach students to build the Church of Christ out of the actual relationships in which they stand to their teachers and to their schoolfellows.

Short Prayers for the Long Day

174

Family Entertainment

Our Father,
we pray that:
Purity replaces innuendos
Charm replaces horror
Gentleness replaces violence
Compassion replaces callousness
Giving replaces greediness
May the teaching of your Son be our
example, always.

R.C.C.

The Motorist's Prayer[11]

GRANT ME a steady hand and a watchful eye
that no man shall be hurt when I pass by.
Thou gavest life, and I pray no act of mine
may take away or mar that gift of Thine.
Shelter those, dear Lord, who bear me
    company
from the evils of fire and all calamity.
Teach me to use my car for others' need,
nor miss through love of speed
the beauties of Thy world; that thus I may
with joy and courtesy go on my way.

Geraldine Binnall

The Emergency Services

WE THANK THEE, heavenly Father, for those who remain awake whilst men sleep.
For doctors and nurses who man the hospitals of our land, relieving pain and comforting the anxious;
For policemen on their lonely patrols, keeping law and order in our society;
For firemen, standing by, ready to rush out to any emergency;
For those who keep the lines of communication open and the wheels of industry turning.

Ronald H. Lloyd

Ageing Gently

LORD THOU KNOWEST better than I know myself that I am growing older and will someday be old. Keep me from the fatal habit of thinking I must say something on every subject and on every occasion. Release me from craving to straighten out everybody's affairs. Make me thoughtful but not moody: helpful but not bossy. With my vast store of wisdom, it seems a pity not to use it all, but thou knowest Lord that I want a few friends at the end.

Keep my mind free from the recital of endless details; give me wings to get to the point. Seal my lips on my aches and pains. They are increasing, and love of rehearsing them is becoming sweeter as the years go by. I dare not ask for grace enough to enjoy the tales of other's pains, but help me to endure them with patience. I dare not ask for improved memory, but for a growing humility and a lessening cocksureness when my memory seems to clash with the memories of others. Teach me the glorious lesson that occasionally I may be mistaken.

Keep me reasonably sweet; I do not want to be a Saint – some of them are so hard to live with – but a sour old person is one of the crowning works of the devil. Give me the ability to see good things in unexpected places, and talents in unexpected people. And, give me, O Lord, the grace to tell them so.

Seventeenth century nun's prayer

Wise Women

LIVE YOUR LIFE while you have it. Life is a splendid gift. There is nothing small in it. For the greatest things grow by God's law out of the smallest. You must not fritter it away in 'fair purpose, erring act, inconstant will'; but must make your thoughts, your words, your acts, all work to the same end, and that end not self, but God. That is what we call *character*.

Florence Nightingale

I WANT TO SEE more fruit of the Spirit in all things, more devotion, more cultivation of mind, more enlargement of heart towards all; more tenderness towards delinquents and, above all, more of the rest, peace and liberty of the children of God.

Elizabeth Fry

Peace

SADAKO WAS a little Japanese girl, badly affected by the Hiroshima bomb. She was taken to hospital for treatment. The nurses encouraged her and other children to accept medication by folding them origami figures out of the small square medicine wrappers. Sadako's favourite figure was the crane: an old Japanese legend said that anyone who faithfully folded 1,000 cranes would have his or her wish fulfilled.

The little girl began folding the cranes herself: her wish was that she should recover. When she sensed that she would never get better, she changed her wish – praying instead for peace between the nations. To every crane she folded, she whispered, 'I will write peace on your wings and you will fly all over the world.' She had folded between 600 and 700 cranes when she died.

The children of Japan learned of Sadako's wish and they, too, began folding cranes. Every year on 6th August, thousands of paper cranes are suspended from the tower in Hiroshima Peace Park.

Kate Compston

IN 1986 a group of American Christians was visiting Russia. After a service in a Russian Orthodox Church, an elderly woman pushed three roubles into the hand of the minister leading the party, Dr Blair Monie, and asked him to buy a candle and light it at his services in his church as a symbol of peace.

When he returned home, Dr Monie duly bought a candle in a glass holder and placed it on the Communion table in the First Presbyterian Church, York, Pennsylvania. This is lit at every service of worship. Later that year, the church decided to buy a supply of candles and holders, inviting members of the congregation to send them to other churches with which they had contact. Two members of that congregation had previously been members of Wylde Green United Reformed Church at Sutton Coldfield, England, and they sent a candle to their former church. Wylde Green URC decided to do likewise ... and now candles are being sent in all directions.

May that old Russian woman's hope of peace be spread far and wide, as churches in many parts of the world receive these reminders of the vital task of working and praying for peace.

Geoffrey Duncan

The Transfiguration of our Lord

(6 August)

JESUS, THE HEALER and teacher of multitudes, turns his face to Jerusalem and death. Before he goes, he climbs high into the hills. He prays, and the cloud touches him. He is transfigured, and what he is, shines out of him. Old saints are visible in his light, conversing with him. It is good to be here; if good for Peter and his companions, how much more blest for Christ, that he should inhabit a mountain hermitage, taken up in God. But men must be illuminated, and from another station; a wooden candlestick on Calvary awaits the light of the world.

Austin Farrer

Love
(based on 1 Corinthians 13)

LOVE IS a whisper,
Not a tornado.
Love is a drift of petals,
Not a mighty oak tree,
Love is the song of a flute,
Not the blast of a trumpet.

Love is a beckoning finger,
Not a pair of handcuffs.
This is its strength.
It invites,
It does not force.
It's like a camp fire.
We gather round,
And are warmed.

Anna Compston (aged 12)

Alienation

Race and Culture

BECAUSE my mouth
is wide with laughter,
and my throat
is deep with song,
you do not think
I suffer after
I have held my pain
so long.
Because my mouth
is wide with laughter,
you do not hear
my inner cry;
because my feet

are gay with dancing,
you do not know
I die.

Langston Hughes

O GOD who has called men and women to
every land to be a holy nation, a royal
priesthood, the Church of your dear Son;
unite us in mutual love across the barriers of
race and culture, and strengthen us in our
common task of being Christ and showing
Christ to the world he came to save.

John Kingsnorth (U.S.P.G.)

ALIENATION has been defined as *being absent in the presence of the other* – absent to
his need, his longing to be accepted as a
person, his search for identity, his joys and
griefs.

A Closer Walk With God

Marriage

A good marriage must be created.
In the marriage, the little things are the big things ...
It is never being too old to hold hands.
It is remembering to say 'I love you' at least once a day,
It is never going to sleep angry.
It is having a mutual sense of values and common objectives.
It is standing together and facing the world.
It is forming a circle of love that gathers in the whole family.
It is speaking words of appreciation and demonstrating gratitude in thoughtful ways.
It is having the capacity to forgive and forget.
It is giving each other an atmosphere in which each can grow.
It is a common search for the good and the beautiful.
It is not only marrying the right person.
It is being the right partner.

Unknown

The Mothers' Union Prayer

ALMIGHTY GOD, our heavenly Father, who gave marriage to be a source of blessing, we thank you for the joys of family life, with all its joys and sorrows.

May we know your presence and peace in our homes, fill them with your love and use them to your glory.

Bless all who are married and every parent and child.

Pour out upon us your Holy Spirit, that we may truly love and serve you.

Bless the members of the Mothers' Union throughout the world, unite us in prayer and worship, in love and service, that, strengthened by your grace, we may seek to do your will; through Jesus Christ, our Lord.

Wedding Anniversary

GRACIOUS GOD, on this our special day we remember with thanksgiving our vows of love and commitment to you and to each other in marriage. We pray for your continued blessing. May we learn from both our joys and sorrows, and discover new riches

185

in our life together in you. We ask this in the name of Jesus Christ our Lord.

Anglican Church of Canada
Alternative Service Book

The Family

A Prayer for the Family

ALMIGHTY GOD, who hast ordained that we should dwell together in families over the face of the earth, and should learn wisdom and grace through the discipline of our homes: Protect we beseech thee, the families of mankind against assaults from without and disloyalties within; and so increase every family in true religion and nourish it in all goodness that its members may abide together in thy peace, continue in thy favour, and finally dwell together in thine eternal kingdom, through Jesus Christ our Lord.

Unknown

A Birthday

GOD OUR FATHER, the birth of your son Jesus Christ brought great joy to Mary and Joseph. We give thanks to you for . . . , whose birthday we celebrate today. May he/she ever grow in your faith, hope, and love. We ask this in the name of our Lord Jesus Christ.

Anglican Church of Canada.
Alternative Service Book

Christian Unity

O GOD, whose will it is that all your children should be one in Christ; we pray for the unity of your Church. Pardon all our pride and our lack of faith, of understanding and of charity, which are the causes of our divisions. Deliver us from narrow-mindedness, from our bitterness, from our prejudices. Save us from considering as normal that which is a scandal to the world and an offence to your love. Teach us to recognize the gifts of grace among all those who call upon you and confess the faith of Jesus Christ our Lord.

French Reformed Church Liturgy

FATHER GOD, we treasure our faith and traditions and those who have helped us on our pilgrimage. In our multi-faith culture, help us to extend reverence and respect to those who hold different ideas and beliefs from our own. Help us to widen our understanding as the world becomes 'smaller'; to listen, learn and share. For it is in these activities that our own beliefs become clearer, which clarifies where we are on our own spiritual journey. It is good for us to take stock of ourselves.

R.C.C.

Civil Strife

ETERNAL RULER and Creator God, stamp out the greed and recklessness that leads to civil strife in your world. Be with the victims of inhumanitarian acts to individuals, families and communities. Banish brutality and extinguish evil.

R.C.C.

The Armed Forces

O GOD our Father, we pray for all those who serve our country as sailors, soldiers and airmen. Grant that meeting danger with courage, and all occasions with discipline and loyalty, they may truly serve the cause of justice and peace, for the honour of your name.

New Every Morning (adapted)

The Homeless

LORD JESUS, poorest of the poor,
born in a borrowed stable
and buried in a borrowed tomb,
I bring before you all those who, like you,
have nowhere to lay their head:
the war refugees exiled from their homes,
migrants searching for a place to live,
the victims of earthquakes, floods and
    disasters,
and the countless, countless homeless in
    this land.
Help me, living as I am securely and in
    peace,
to show compassion for my brothers and
    sisters,

and help them find in their lives
a new beginning and new hope,
for your name's sake.

H.J. Richards[12]

The Big Issue Magazine

HE WAS SELLING copies of the *Big Issue* and stood pressed against a wall, as the Christmas shoppers streamed by. He was very young and inadequately dressed for the rawness of the fog. His bald head and pony tail seemed to emphasise the rings in his nose and ears. But it was he who gave me the most memorable Christmas present of the year. His smile. It transformed him. His face shone from the very heart of God when asked to keep the change for a cup of tea; before returning to his roof of cardboard. Pray for him, and those like him, around the world.

R.C.C.

Responsible Journalism

WE PRAY for those who job it is to report the news about communities, regions and nations. Father God, guide the endeavours of journalists and broadcasters so that they may recognise their responsibilities of power and privilege. May they value truth, accuracy, justice and privacy. Empower them with grace, energy and wisdom so that good news continues to be news!

R.C.C.

A Blessing

GO, AND KNOW that the Lord goes with you: let him lead you each day into the quiet place of your heart, and where he will speak with you; know that he loves you and watches over you – that he listens to you in gentle understanding, that he is with you always, wherever you are and however you may feel: and the blessing of God – Father, Son and Holy Spirit – be yours for ever.

Still Waters, Deep Waters

191

7

FROM EARTH TO HEAVEN

Faith

IN QUIETNESS and in trust shall be your strength

Isaiah 30 v 15, RSV

FAITH IS putting one's foot down in the mist and finding it on a rock.

Anon

IF GOD SENDS us on stony paths he provides strong shoes.

Corrie ten Boom

FAITH IS to believe what you do not yet see; the reward for this faith is to see what you believe.

St Augustine

AND ALMOST everyone when age,
Disease, or sorrow strike him,
Inclines to think there is a God,
Or something very like him.

Arthur Hugh Clough

The Next Life

THIS WORLD is given us as an inn in which to stay, but not to dwell.

Cicero

DEATH IS the one single issue about which we are condemned to ignorance, and yet it is the one issue about which we most long for knowledge. This is the great paradox of life.

Funerals: A Guide

ONE MUST take all one's life to learn how to live, and ... one must take all one's life to learn how to die.

Seneca

SINCE IT is possible that you may depart from this life at this very moment, regulate every act and thought accordingly.

Marcus Aurelius

I BELIEVE it is of real value to our earthly life to have the next life in mind, because if we shut it out of our thoughts we are starving part of our spiritual nature – we are like children who fail to grow up – none the finer children for that. Not only do we miss much joy in the earth life if we imagine it to be the whole of our existence, but we arrive on the further shore with no knowledge of the language of the new country where we shall find ourselves unfitted for the large life of the spirit.

Joan Mary Fry

THE LIFE that I have
Is all that I have
And the life that I have is yours.

The love that I have
Of the life that I have
Is yours and yours and yours.

A sleep I shall have
Yet death will be but a pause.

For the peace of my years
In the long green grass
Will be yours and yours.

Leo Marks

Time

Ordering Crosses

CROSSES ARE never what we ordered, but always either greater than we ordered, smaller than we ordered, or other than we ordered – and it does not matter much which; for God measures the love with which they are carried, and not the poundage of each particular weight.

Austin Farrer

WHEN AS A CHILD I laughed and wept –
Time crept
When as a youth I waxed more bold –
Time strolled
When I became a full grown man –
Time ran
When older still I grew –
Time flew
Soon I shall find in passing on –
Time gone
O Christ wilt Thou have saved me then –

Anon

THROUGH EVERY minute of this day,
Be with me, Lord!
Through every day of all this week
Be with me, Lord!
Through every week of all this year
Be with me, Lord!
Through all the years of all this life,
Be with me, Lord!
So shall the days and weeks and years
Be threaded on a golden cord.
And all draw on with sweet accord
Unto thy fulness, Lord
That so, when time is past,
By grace I may at last,
Be with thee, Lord.

John Oxenham

Ageing

LORD, I AM growing old.
I am slower than I used to be.
My memory is not so good.
The disabilities and irritations
of old age come upon me.
I find myself telling the same old jokes.
Loved ones and friends pass on

across the frontier of this life and the
next.
Lord God, I dare to ask in prayer
if I may keep in touch with them and
they with me.
May your beloved Son,
who brings love to us,
take our love to them,
for he still spans this world of creation
and the world of full life.

George Appleton

JUST A LINE to say I'm living -
That I'm not among the dead,
Though I'm getting more forgetful
And mixed up in the head.
I've got used to my arthritis
To my dentures I'm resigned,
I can cope with my bi-focals,
But – ye gods – I miss my mind!
Sometimes I can't remember
When I'm standing by the stair,
If I'm going up for something
Or have just come down from there.
And before the fridge so often
My mind is full of doubt:
Now did I put some food away –
Or have I come to take some out?

So, remember, I do love you,
And wish that you lived near.
And now it's time to post this
And say goodbye, my dear.

At last I stand beside the postbox
And my face – I'm sure it's red –
Instead of posting this to you,
I've opened it instead!

Anon (adapted)

DURING EACH life period, a new measure of the Word of God must be built, living stone by stone, into the very structure of the growing personality, just as the energy of the sun is built into the plants of the earth. Childhood, adolescence, maturity, middle age and old age, each and every phase of life calls for the discovery of new potentialities within the eternal self ... Thus, by a process of growth, the healthy spirit is prepared for the last crisis, death, when the body returns to the earth, and the spirit to God who gave it. If the spirit be in health, the fate of its tabernacle becomes of slight concern ...

Stephen Grellet

WITH MIRTH and laughter let old wrinkles come.

William Shakespeare

LOOK FOR ME in the nurseries of heaven.

Francis Thompson

Nursing the Elderly

HE WAS A CHILD before we were born –
Now he is helpless, old and forlorn.
He was a husband long years ago,
He walked with his wife, their cheeks all
   aglow.
His wife was a mother; she had babes at
   her breast,
Caring for others, and giving her best.
He was a man, salute him for this,
Now he is withered, and harder to kiss.
Speak to him gently, and nurse him with
   pride,
Now, as he waits to sail with the tide.
Ours are the last hands he'll ever hold.
Let him know love, now he is old.

Kathy Doyle

House Communion

WEEKDAY sunlight
streaming on to the
Holy Table,
and you're there.
Unemployed.
A blessing!

'Blessed is He that
comes in the name of
The Lord'
and you're there.
Mind-full.
A blessing!

'Could you not
watch with me
one brief hour?'
and you're there.
Able-to-kneel.
A blessing!

Holy Saturday:
'The Light of Christ!'
'Thanks be to God!'
and you're there.
Hearing.
A blessing!

The Easter dawn, and its
Resurrection joy with
earth and heaven united,
and you're there.
Believing.
A blessing!

Come ye thankful people
raise the song of
harvest home,
and you're there.
Sensing and singing.
A blessing!

Awaiting the priest's car
and his knock
with the Holy Feast.
You're there, and
our prayers come too
with His Blessing.

R.C.C.
For my mother, Easter 1996

Holy Unction

Is ANY AMONG you sick? Call for the elders of the church to pray over you and anoint you with oil in the name of the Lord. And the prayer offered in faith will make you well; the Lord will raise you up. If you have sinned, you will be forgiven. Therefore confess your sins to each other and pray for each other so that you may be healed. The prayer of a righteous person is powerful and effective.

James 5 v 14–16, NIV

As WITH visible oil your body outwardly is anointed, so our heavenly Father, Almighty God, grant of his infinite goodness that your soul inwardly may be anointed with the Holy Ghost, who is the Spirit of all strength, relief and gladness. May he, according to his blessed will, restore to you full strength and health of body, mind and spirit that you may withstand all temptations and in Christ's victory triumph over evil, sin and death: through Jesus Christ our Lord, who by his death hath overcome the prince of death; and with the Father and the Holy Spirit evermore liveth and reigneth God, world without end.

Western Rite of Anointing

WE ARE IN 1903 and I am nearly seventy-one years old. I always thought I should love to grow old, and I find it is even more delightful than I thought. It is so delicious to be done with things, and to feel no need any longer to concern myself much about earthly affairs. I seem on the verge of a most delightful journey to a place of unknown joys and pleasures, and things here seem of so little importance compared to things there, that they have lost most of their interest for me.

I cannot describe the sort of done-with-the-world feeling I have. It is not that I feel as if I was going to die at all, but simply that the world seems to me nothing but a passage way to the real life beyond; and passage ways are very unimportant places. It is of very little account what sort of things they contain, or how they are furnished. One just hurries through them to get to the place beyond.

My wants seem to be gradually narrowing down, my personal wants, I mean, and I often think I could be quite content in the Poor-house! I do not know whether this is piety or old age, or a little of each mixed together, but honestly the world and our life in it does seem of too little account to be worth making the least fuss over, when one has such a magnificent prospect close at hand ahead of one; and I am tremendously content to let one activity after another go, and to await quietly and happily the opening of the door at the end of the passage way, that will let me in to my real abiding place. So you may think of me as happy and contented, surrounded with unnumbered blessings, and delighted to be seventy-one years old.

Ed. Logan Pearsall Smith

Being Alone

ALONE WITH none but thee, my God,
I journey on my way.
What need I fear, when thou art near
O king of night and day?
More safe am I within thy hand
Than if a host did round me stand.

Columba

I HAVE NO FEAR of death – but I shall welcome a helping hand to see me through.
For it is said that just as everyone has a

guardian angel, so to each one comes somebody to help us over the stile.

Once I am over, I know a door will open a new loveliness and freshness of colour, form and light which is far more beautiful than anything I have ever seen or imagined.

Praying for Others

WATCH, DEAR LORD,
with those who wake, or watch, or
   weep tonight,
and give your angels charge over
   those who sleep.
Tend your sick ones, O Lord Christ,
rest your weary ones,
bless your dying ones,
soothe your suffering ones,
pity your afflicted ones,
shield your joyous ones,
I ask all this for your love's sake.

St Augustine

SURELY THE 'tender bridge' that joins the living and the dead in Christ is prayer. Mutual intercession is the life-blood of the fellowship, and what is there in a Christian's death that can possibly check its flow? To ask for the prayers of others in this life, and to know that they rely on mine, does not show any lack of faith in the all-sufficiency of God. Then, in the same faith, let me ask for their prayers still, and offer mine for them, even when death has divided us. They pray for me, I believe, with clearer understanding, but I for them in ignorance, though still with love. And love, not knowledge, is the substance of prayer.

Funerals: A Guide

Preparing for Heaven

AS THE RAIN hides the stars
As the autumn mist hides the hills
As the clouds veil the blue of the sky
So the dark happenings of my lot
Hide the shining of thy face from me.
Yet, if I might hold thy hand in the darkness it
    is enough.
Since I know that though I may stumble in my
    going thou dost not fall.

The Oxford Book of Prayer

Christz

CHRIST IS that bright morning star,
which, when the light of this world fails,
   bringeth his saints to the joy of eternal life,
and to the light of everlasting day.

Venerable Bede

GOD BE WITH YOU till we meet again,
By his counsels guide, uphold you,
With his sheep securely fold you:
God be with you till we meet again.

God be with you till we meet again,
'Neath his wings protecting hide you,
Daily manna still provide you:
God be with you till we meet again.

God be with you till we meet again,
When life's perils thick confound you,
Put his arms unfailing round you:
God be with you till we meet again.

God be with you till we meet again,
Keep love's banner floating o'er you,
Smile death's threatening wave before
   you:
God be with you till we meet again.

Jeremiah Eames Rankin

Farewell

Do Not Stand At My Grave[13]

DO NOT STAND at my grave and weep
I am not there. I do not sleep.
I am a thousand winds that blow
I am the diamond glints on snow.
I am the sunlight on ripened grain
I am the gentle autumn rain.
When you awaken in the morning's hush
I am the swift uplifting rush
of quiet birds in circled flight.
I am the soft stars that shine at night.
Do not stand at my grave and cry,
I am not there; I do not die.

So HEED, hear when you awaken what I say,
I live with you and guard your way.

Funerals: a Guide

The Happy Mourning

AU REVOIR, I say, au revoir
Not farewell or goodbye
But au revoir –
The day has come for you
The day will come for me –
See you on that day

With happiness around –
God is good to me
He has been good to you
Thank you Lord for feelings,
For sadness for life
Au revoir, I say au revoir
Not farewell, not goodbye,
But au revoir and
thanks –

J.P.I. Tyson, 1984
a grandchild

* * *

A Service in Dunblane Cathedral
17 March 1996[14]

Offertory Prayer

LORD GOD, it is little we have to bring you today. The gifts from out of our wealth, but also the poverty of our faith and the brokenness of our spirit. Yet what we have we lay before you, trusting you to redeem and transform all that we are and to touch us once more with your life. Through Jesus Christ our Lord who taught us when we pray, to say, Our Father …

Hymn

WE CANNOT measure how you heal
or answer every sufferer's prayer
Yet we believe your grace responds
where faith and doubt unite to care.

Your hands, though bloodied on the cross,
Survive to hold and heal and warn.
To carry all through death to life
And cradle children yet unborn.

The pain that will not go away,
The guilt that clings from things long past,
The fear of what the future holds
Are present as if meant to last.

But present, too, is love which tends
The hurt we never hoped to find,
The private agonies inside,
The memories that haunt the mind.

So some have come who need your help
And some have come to make amends
As hands which shaped and saved the world
Are present in the touch of friends.

Lord, let your Spirit meet us here
To mend the body, mind and soul,
To disentangle peace from pain
And make your broken people whole.

John Bell and Graham Maule

'FEAR NOT' says the Lord 'for I am with you.
Be not dismayed for I am your God. I will
strengthen you, I will help you, I will uphold
you with the hand of my righteousness.'

God, our Father, listen to us this day.
Your troubled and anxious people.
We need your Presence.
We need your peace.
We need the assurance of your love with
    us still.
Our thoughts today overwhelm us.
Words are hard to find,
but you are there in the whole of life –
its beginning and its ending.

So help us to find you in our pain,
as many times past we have known you in
    our joy.
That in all our confusing thoughts,
in our gratitude and our grief
we may know that you still hold us,
and you understand us and you will see us
    through.

Lord God, at the moment of our falling hold
us and save us in Jesus Christ.

Lord God, when there's ultimate loneliness be present to befriend us in Jesus Christ.

Lord God, when our private world is in chaos enable us to see the way ahead in Jesus Christ.

Lord God, when the shadow of death is near us give us the life which is in Jesus Christ.

God of all peace, calm our troubled and anxious souls for you are with us here and you will heal all our hurts through Jesus Christ our Lord, we pray. Amen.

Address (extract) to the
Sunday School children

AND WHEN we are feeling like that – sad, confused and frightened – you know it's not wrong to cry and it's not wrong to tell people how we feel; and it's not wrong to remember all the good times we had with our friends, and to smile as we remember. And today I want us to smile as we remember all the very special things about our friends.

Do you know what people sometimes do when they're feeling sad, or afraid, or just feeling very, very lonely? They hold hands.

Because when you hold someone else's hand it means that you're not alone. It means that there's someone there who can share things with you.

To hold someone else's hand means that someone else is supporting you and helping you through a difficult time. And so people often hold hands with each other.

There's a story in the Bible about Jesus and the children. It says that when the children came to Jesus he took them up in his arms and he put his hands upon them. Jesus used his hands.

And you know I think that when Jesus did that these children must have felt so very, very safe because when someone holds your hand it means that they are caring for you and will always protect you, and that we are safe.

And I want us to think that today we are very, very safe because we can put our hand into someone else's hand – a parent, or our grandparent or our friends, or everyone else who is here in Dunblane and cares for us and will always protect us.

And so this morning as we remember the children I want to read their names. I want us to remember how special they were. And as you do that I want you to hold hands. Hold hands with whoever is sitting beside you and everyone in the church today can do the same.

Hold hands and remember that we all are helping each other and remember that love means we're safe. And as we read the names we will think about our special friends. How special they were. Then we'll have a moment's silence and then we'll say a prayer ...

Hymn

Goodness is stronger than evil;
Love is stronger than hate;
Light is stronger than darkness;
Life is stronger than death;
Vict'ry is ours, Vict'ry is ours,
through him who loved us.

Desmond Tutu

Hymn

O FATHER on your love we call,
When sorrow overshadows all,
And pain that feels too great to bear
Drives from us any words for prayer;
Enfold in love for evermore
All those we love, but see no more.

Our children, innocent and dear,
Were strangers to a world of fear;
Each precious life had more to give,
In each, our hopes and dreams could live;
Enfold in love for evermore
All those we love, but see no more.

So brief, the joy since each were born,
So long the years in which to mourn;
Give us compassion to sustain
Each other in this time of pain;
Enfold in love for evermore
All those we love, but see no more.

Guard us from bitterness and hate,
And share with us grief's crushing weight
Help us to live from day to day,
Until, once more, we find our way;
Enfold in love for evermore
All those we love, but see no more.

When dark despair is all around,
And falling tears the only sound,
Light one small flame of hope that still
You walk with us and always will
Enfold in love for evermore
All those we love, but see no more.

Jean Holloway

* * *

God's Loan

'I'LL LEND YOU, for a little while
a child of mine' God said,
'For you to cherish while (s)he lives
and mourn for her when (s)he's dead.
It may be six or seven years,
or twenty-two or three,
but will you, 'till I call her/him home
look after her/him for me?

'(S)He will bring her/his love to gladden you
and should her/his stay be brief,
you'll have a host of memories
as solace for your grief.
I cannot promise (s)he will stay,
since all from earth return
but there are lessons taught below
I want this child to learn.

'I've looked the whole world over
in my search for teachers true,
and from the throng that crowds life's lanes
at last I've chosen you.
Now will you give her/him all my love,
nor think your labour vain,
or turn against me when I come
to take her/him back again?'

I fancied that I heard them say
'Dear God, thy will be done'
For all the joy this child will bring
the risk of grief we'll run
We will shelter her/him with tenderness,
we will love her/him while we may
And for the happiness we've known
forever grateful stay.

'But should the angels call her/him home
much sooner than we planned,
we'll brave the bitter grief that comes
and try to understand.'

* * *

Sent to the community of Dunblane in an expression of sympathy

Tears

WHEN WE are dead, and people weep for us and grieve, let it be because we touched their lives with beauty and simplicity.
Let it not be said that life was good to us, but, rather, that we were good to life.

Funerals: a Guide

DEATH IS NOT the extinguishing of the light,
but the putting out of the lamp, because
Dawn has come.

Rabindranath Tagore

TO LIVE in hearts we leave is not to die.

Thomas Campbell

Remembering

REMEMBER ME when I am gone away,
Gone far away into the silent land;
When you can no more hold me by the
    hand,
Nor I half turn to go, yet turning stay.
Remember me when no more day by day
You tell me of our future that you'd planned:
Only remember me; you understand
It will be late to counsel then or pray.
Yet if you should forget me for a while
And afterwards remember, do not grieve:
For if the darkness and corruption leave
A vestige of the thoughts that once I had,
Better by far you should forget and smile
Than that you should remember and be sad.

Christina Georgina Rossetti

SO JUST AS a good mariner when he draws near to the harbour lets down his sails, and enters it gently with slight headway on; so we ought to let down the sails of our worldly pursuits, and turn to God with all our understanding and heart, so that we may come to that haven with all composure and with all peace. And our own nature gives us a good lesson in gentleness, in so far as there is in such a depth no pain, nor any bitterness; but as a ripe apple lightly and without violence detaches itself from its bough, so our soul severs itself without suffering from the body where it has dwelt.

Dante

I AM STANDING upon that foreshore. A ship at my side spreads her white sails to the morning breeze and starts for the blue ocean. She is an object of beauty and strength and I stand and watch until at length she hangs like a speck of white cloud just where the sea and sky come down to mingle with each other. Then someone at my side says, 'There! She's gone!' 'Gone where?' 'Gone from my sight, that's all.' She is just as large in mast and spar and hull as ever she was when she left my side; just as able to bear her load of living freight to the place of her destination. Her diminished size is in me, not in her. And just at that moment when someone at my side says, 'There! She's gone!' there are other eyes watching her coming and other voices ready to take up the glad shout, 'Here she comes!' And that is dying.

Funerals: A Guide

Victory

THINE BE the glory, risen, conquering Son,
Endless is the victory thou o'er death hast
    won;
Angels in bright raiment rolled the stone
    away,
Kept the folded grave-clothes where the
    body lay.
Thine be the glory, risen conquering Son,
Endless is the victory thou o'er death hast
    won.

Lo, Jesus meets us, risen from the tomb;
Lovingly he greets us, scatters fear and
 gloom;
Let the Church with gladness hymns of
 triumph sing,
For her Lord now liveth, death hast lost its
 sting:
Thine be the glory, risen, conquering Son,
Endless is the victory thou o'er death hast
 won.

No more we doubt thee, glorious Prince of
 Life;
Life is nought without thee: aid us in our
 strife,
Make us more than conquerors through thy
 deathless love;
Bring us safe through Jordan to thy home
 above:
Thine be the glory, risen, conquering Son,
Endless is the victory thou o'er death hast
 won.

                                Edmund Budry

DEATH IS nothing at all. I have only slipped
away into the next room. I am I and you are
you. Whatever we were to each other, that we
are still. Call me by my old familiar name,
speak to me in the easy way you always used.
Put no difference into your tone, wear no
forced air of solemnity or sorrow ... What is
death but a negligible accident? Why should I
be out of mind because I am out of sight? I am
waiting for you, for an interval, somewhere
very near just around the corner. All is well.

Henry Scott Holland

GO FORTH upon thy journey, Christian soul!
Go from this world! Go, in the name of God
The omnipotent Father who created thee!
Go, in the name of Jesus Christ, our Lord,
Son of the living God, who bled for thee!
Go, in the name of the Holy Spirit, who
Hath been poured out on thee! Go, in the
    name
Of Angels and Archangels; in the name
Of Thrones and Dominations; in the name
Of Princedoms and of Powers; and in the
    name
Of Cherubim and Seraphim, go forth!
Go, in the name of Patriarchs and Prophets;
And of Apostles and Evangelists,

Of Martyrs and Confessors; in the name
Of Holy Monks and Hermits; in the name
Of holy virgins; and all Saints of God,
Both men and women, go! Go on thy
  course!
And may thy place today be found in peace,
And may thy dwelling be the Holy Mount
Of Sion: through the same, through Christ,
  our Lord.

J. H. Newman

The 1995 Church Survey

From St George's Day
Sunday 23 April to
Saturday 29 April
with the kind help of
THE GUIDE AND SCOUT ASSOCIATIONS

Of the one million registered blind and partially sighted people 220,000 regularly attend church/church groups. Your help by visiting every denominational church in England to discover what provision, if any, has been made for them will help to ensure that their needs are widely known. Through your thorough observation we hope that their spiritual alienation will soon cease. Thank you so much for your help.

QUESTIONS

1. Does this place of worship have some large-print hymn books?
2. Does this place of worship have some large-print service books?
3. Does this building have large print tourist guides?
4. Are indoor and outside steps edged with white paint?
5. Does this place of worship have a hymn book in braille?
6. Does this place of worship have a service book in braille?
7. Do the clergy provide all *Special Service Sheets* in large print? e.g. Carol, Family, Harvest, Ordination, Enthronement Services?
8. Are Pew Sheets, Weekly Notices, Menus produced in large print?

9. Are Church magazines and Diocesan Newspapers recorded on audio tape?

10. Are the first lines of hymns announced for those who rely on memory?

Church House, Westminster received the 2,864 completed surveys.

Notes

1. The importance of the appropriate literary provision for full participation in worship – whereby those present are welcomed in Maori and then in English – cannot be overemphasised. New Zealand's example is a source of encouragement as the opening words of every Holy Communion service are to the Maoris, although they are not generally expected to be there.

2. The seven sacraments (some Christians recognise only two) are an outward visible sign of an inward grace.

3. A prayer used by the Iona Community at the start of each weekly pilgrimage around the island.

4. Sung at the Requiem Mass in Southwell Minster, on 19 March, for Eric Brandreth Freckingham 1901–96.

5. With permission of Professor John M. Hull, founder of Cathedrals by Touch and Hearing, from his book *Touching the Rock* about his experience of blindness. It is available on audio tape and in braille from the RNIB, address below. The book is now entitled: *On Sight and Insight: A Journey Into the World of Blindness*. It is hoped that anyone connected with the Church will read it.

6. Anne Frank, 5 April 1944, aged 15, in hiding in Holland.

7. From *The Rite Lines*, the quarterly newsletter of Broken Rites, an independent association of divorced and separated

wives of Anglican clergy and ministers of non-established Churches, living in the United Kingdom.

8. Worldwide, there are forty-two million blind and partially-sighted people.

9. A love-feast held by early Christians in connection with the Lord's Supper. The prayer was given to me by the Revd Leonard Lord shortly before his death in 1992.

10. See address below for the Guide Dogs for the Blind Association.

11. In the United Kingdom in 1991, a police traffic survey estimated that three and a half million drivers had defective eyesight.

12. In 1996, one person in every hundred is a refugee. In the United Kingdom, four million are without work, and an unknown (uncounted) number are homeless.

13. Left by Stephen Cummins, a soldier killed in Northern Ireland.

14. On Wednesday 13 March 1996, sixteen children aged five and their teacher were massacred in their primary school at Dunblane, Scotland. Four days later, on Mothering Sunday, a one-minute silence was honoured throughout the British Isles at 9.30 a.m. as families, friends, colleagues, and the nation attempted to express their sympathy, bewilderment and grief. Shortly afterwards a service was relayed live on television by BBC Scotland.

Additional Information

1. The Partially Sighted Society,
63 Salusbury Road,
London NW6 6RH.
Tel: 0171–372 1551 (ansaphone)

2. Torch Trust for the Blind,
Torch House, Hallaton,
Market Harborough,
Leics LE16 8UJ.
Tel: 01858–555 301

3. The Royal National Institute for the Blind (RNIB),
Customer Services,
PO Box 173,
Peterborough PE2 6WS.
Tel: 0345–023 153

4. Guide Dogs for the Blind Association,
Hillfields,
Burghfields,
Reading,
Berkshire RG7 3YG.
Tel: 01734–835 555

Sources

While every effort has been made to contact owners of copyright material, there are some who have not been traced. The author and publishers gratefully acknowledge the following copyright owners whose material appears in this book with permission.

John Betjeman, 'Blame the Vicar', *Church Poems*, John Murray (Publishers) Ltd used with kind permission.

Simone Weil, *Waiting on God* (Collins/Fontana, 1951) used with kind permission of Routledge Ltd.

Father Anthony OSB, Benedictine Spirituality, used with kind permission.

Scripture quotations marked 'RSV' are taken from the Revised Standard Version of the Bible, copyright 1946, 1952, 1971, by the Division of Christian Education of the National Council of the Churches of Christ in the USA. Used by permission. Other

230

HarperCollins Publishers
Giles and Melville Harcourt, *Short Prayers for the Long Day*; Harold Winstone, *The Sunday Missal*; John P Dewis, *The Daily Missal*; Esther de Waal, *Seeking God the Benedictine Way*; New Zealand Church, *A New Zealand Prayer Book*; Thora Hird, *Praise Be! Book of Prayers*. Clemency Greatorex, 'Martha's Prayer' and 'Teach us to listen' from the *Praise Be! Book of Prayers*. Used with permission.

D.H.Lawrence, 'Shadows' from *The Complete Poems*, with kind permission of Laurence Pollinger Limited and the Estate of Frieda Lawrence Ravagli. 'Shadows' by D. H. Lawrence, from *The Complete Poems of D H Lawrence by D. H. Lawrence*, edited by V de Sola Pinto & F. W. Roberts. Copyright (c) 1964, 1971 by Angelo Ravagli and C. M. Weekley, Executors of the Estate of Frieda Lawrence Ravagli. Used by permission of Viking Penguin, a division of Penguin Books USA Inc.

Judith Sequeira, 'Focus on Christ' ('My Cross', *God's Image* vol 10 No 2 1991 Summer) with permission from the Asian Women's Resource Centre for Culture and Theology, Kuala Lumpur. 'Victims of Society' (c) Harold Williams, Christian Conference of Asia. 'Across the barriers that divide', World Council of Churches, Geneva, Switzerland. 'My mother's name is worry' by a 12 year old child in a slum area, from *Reading the Bible as Asian Women* (c) Christian Conference of Asia. Shirley Erena Murray (c) 'Faith has set us on a journey', with permission of the author and of (c) Hope Publishing Co. administered by Copy Care PO Box 77, Hailsham, East Sussex BN27 SEF. David Clark, 'Companions Let us Pray Together', written for the National Gay Christian Conference, 1991 New Zealand. Janet Lees, 'A Child Asked Me', used with kind permission. Donald Hilton reproduced from *A Word in Season* compiled by Donald Hilton with the permission of the National Christian Education Council. Ronald Grimes, *Lifeblood of Public Ritual*, American University Press used by permission. Kate Compston, 'Sadako', Anna Compston, 'Love', 'Borneo, The Forest' and Geoffrey Duncan 'In 1986', all

233